STEP-BY-STEP GARDEN GUIDES

Leo B. Boullemier

Fuchsias

AURA

Step-by-Step Garden Guides Fuchsias

Leo B. Boullemier

© 1996 Aura Books plc
Produced for Aura Books
by Transedition Ltd,
Oxford OX4 4DJ, England

Editing:
Asgard Publishing Services, Leeds
Typesetting:
Organ Graphic, Abingdon

Photographic credits
All photographs by the author except
as follows: A. Cooper 47 top left; I.
Drapkin 6; E. Goulding 23; Dr M.
Guffy 22, 48; C. Hassett 8; R. Kemp 4,
45, 81 bottom left; Photos
Horticultural 51, 70, 70–71, 80, 82,
83 bottom right, 84–85; F. Snelling 40
bottom

10 9 8 7 6 5
Printed in Dubai

ISBN 0 947793 85 2

Leo B. Boullemier is a past president
of the British Fuchsia Society and a BFS
Senior National Accredited Judge. He
has been a specialist fuchsia grower
for more decades than he cares to
remember. In addition to regular
gardening magazine columns, he has
written numerous books on fuchsias,
including the definitive reference work
Checklist of the Genus Fuchsia, which
lists and describes all reported species,
sub-species, varieties and cultivars.
   In 1987 Mr Boullemier was awarded
the Whiteman Medal of Honour by the
British Fuchsia Society. The highest
honour in the fuchsia world, this medal
is awarded only rarely, in recognition
of outstanding services to the fuchsia.

CONTENTS

'Montrose Village'

Why grow fuchsias?

It isn't difficult to see why the fuchsia has gained so much popularity in the garden. Whether it's under glass or out in the open it will always stand out from the other plants, providing a continuous display of flowers throughout the summer.

Fuchsias flower freely, and their exotic blooms are often described as 'ballerinas' or 'dancing ladies'. Thousands of cultivars are available, and there are any number of ways to train them. They're easy to cultivate, too: any good, fertile soil will suit their needs, and given moist conditions and a moist atmosphere they will flourish to near perfection.

You can propagate fuchsias at any time of year, provided the conditions are right. Their cuttings root more easily than most, and a greenhouse is not essential. A fuchsia laden with delicate and graceful blooms is one of the most elegant and exquisite of all plants, whether grown as a bush, as a standard, trailing or in a basket. Probably the real reason why so many people grow the fuchsia is that it needs so little attention and yet produces such satisfying results.

Lots of fuchsias together can provide a beautiful and impressive display.

Equally breathtaking can be the beauty of just one flower — here 'Bella Rosella'.

5

The treasure of Santo Domingo

Contrary to popular belief, the fuchsia is not an old-fashioned English flower; indeed, less than 200 years ago it was unknown in Britain.

Fuchsias are first mentioned in the 14th and 15th centuries, when the Incas in Peru were cultivating the species *F. boliviana* for edible berries. Even so, fuchsias did not come to the attention of the western world until the late 17th century. Between 1689 and 1697 Father Carole Plumier, a Minim monk and one of the eminent botanists of his day, was looking for cinchona trees — the trees are a source of quinine, used in the treatment of malaria. In the foothills of Santo Domingo he found an unusual plant with scarlet flowers and coppery-bronze foliage. In 1703 he named it *Fuchsia triphylla flore coccinea* after Dr Fuchs, a celebrated German botanist.

Fuchsia triphylla was lost to the world until 1773, when seeds found by the American, William Hogg, were sent to Kew Gardens in England. In 1788 a Captain Firth sent a *F. magellanica* plant to Kew from Brazil, naming it as *F. coccinea*; this was the first plant to reach

England. During the early 19th century several more species were discovered, mainly on the western slopes of the Andes in South America.

In 1832 Bunney of Stratford, London, recorded the first British hybrid when he crossed *F. coccinea* with *F. microphylla* to obtain 'Globosa'.

In 1844 the Frenchman Felix Porcher published the first list of fuchsias, with some 300 entries. Hybridising continued in Britain and France, and in 1848 William Storey of Newton Abbot produced 'Striata', the first striped cultivar. Two years later he produced the first double-flowered cultivars, 'Duplex' and 'Multiplex', and in 1855 the first fuchsias with white petals, 'Mrs Storey' and 'Queen Victoria'.

French growers such as Crousse (1853) and Rozain-Boucharlat (1860) were also producing hybrids, and by the beginning of the 20th century the famous Victor Lemoine had produced 460 different cultivars. There were many English hybridists in the 1850s and 1860s: Banks, Bland, Bull and Harrison produced many of the cultivars still grown today, including 'Mauve Beauty', 'Rose of Castile', 'Rose of Denmark' and 'Lustre'.

The Victorians adored fuchsias. In their heyday (around 1875–1890) every household of note had a collection, and 30–40 new introductions were being raised every year. The colours were mainly red and purple, and in the early days the so-called doubles were really semi-doubles. No history of fuchsias can afford to forget James Lye of Trowbridge, who began to hybridise in 1860. By 1889 he had produced 82 cultivars, including the well-

Planted in 1899 in Ventura, California, this is the oldest fuchsia in the world and still growing.

known (and still grown) 'Amy Lye', 'Charming', 'Duchess of Albany' and 'Scarcity'. He was also a champion fuchsia grower, exhibiting pillars and pyramids 8-10 ft (2.5-3 m) high.

Another breakthrough occurred in 1888, with 'Countess of Aberdeen'. This cultivar by Cocker is almost entirely white, and still one of the best. The Germans began hybridising in 1895 using *F. triphylla* crossed with other species. As a result Bonstedt produced 'Mary' (1894) 'Thalia' (1905) and 'Gartenmeister Bonstedt' (1905), all now very famous.

From the 1890s the popularity of the fuchsia declined. After World War I there was a general rebellion against all things Victorian, and the fuchsia fell completely out of favour.

Even so, the years before World War II saw the birth of two societies that have since become famous. In 1929 fuchsia growers working in California founded the American Fuchsia Society, and in 1938 the British Fuchsia Society was formed as the plant struggled to recover its former glory.

The Americans were very active hybridists, soon producing as many as 40 cultivars every year. By 1975 the figure was closer to 85, and later reached more than 100.

The English hybridists took up the challenge, and the work of Travis, Thornley, Dr Ryle, Gadsby, Roe and Wright created hundreds of new introductions.

The latest revision of the *Checklist of the Genus Fuchsia* (compiled by the author) identifies more than 10,000 species, hybrids and cultivars. Hybridising has declined somewhat in America, but still flourishes in other parts of the world, particularly Britain and Holland.

'Countess of Aberdeen' was the first-ever white fuchsia cultivar, and is still one of the best.

The fuchsia

Fuchsia is one of 21 plant genera within the family Onagraceae, and the most important genus from the ornamental point of view. It is closely related to evening primrose, willow herb, clarkia, godetia and enchanter's nightshade.

Fuchsias are woody plants that prefer temperate or subtropical climates. In their native habitat they produce shrubs and trees. In the UK they produce hardy or half-hardy deciduous shrubs.

'Amy Marie' — a lovely example of a double-flowered cultivar with more than one flower colour.

Terms used in classification

Species: closely related plants of a single kind, distinguished from other species by definable characteristics; a sub-division of a genus. The word 'species' is both singular and plural.

Variety: A natural sub-group that can be distinguished within a species, not so different that it is regarded as a distinct species; any variation within a species.

Hybrid: plant resulting from a cross between genetically different parents; offspring produced by crossing two different species or varieties.

Cultivar: previously known as a 'cultivated variety', and sometimes confused with varieties. Cultivars are a group of clearly distinguishable cultivated plants, produced by crossing species with hybrids or hybrids with hybrids. Most of the fuchsias available from hybridists and nurserymen are cultivars.

Fuchsia flowers are classified as:

Singles: flowers with only four petals.

Semi-doubles: an intermediate category; the flowers have five to eight petals, but cannot be classified as full doubles.

Doubles: flowers with layers of eight or more petals.

Sometimes the tube, sepals and corolla are all the same colour; a flower like this is described as *self-coloured* or a *self*. A typical example is 'Rufus', a turkey-red self. More usually the tube and sepals are one colour and the corolla is a different colour. 'Martin Glow', for instance, has a pure waxy-white tube and sepals and a rich purple corolla. In some cultivars all three parts are different colours. 'Blue Waves' has a very pale pink tube, neyron-rose sepals, and a deep campanula-violet corolla. A few cultivars

A fuchsia flower with all the different parts shown.

don't fit into any category: 'Checkerboard' has a long red tube, a deeper red corolla, and sepals that are red to start with but change abruptly to white.

The parts of a flower

The flower is attached to the *axil* (the angle between the leaf and the stem of the plant) by a stalk known as the *pedicel*. This swells out to form the *ovary*, or berry, which will contain the seeds when it matures. Next comes a similar but much larger section called the *tube* or *hypanthium*, which varies in length and thickness. The tube ends in four segments called *sepals*. Before the bud opens these enclose the flower, but

when it reaches maturity they *recurve* (curl away from the flower) or *reflex* (sweep up and lie around the tube, sometimes hiding it completely). There should be four sepals to each flower. The tube and sepals together are referred to as the *calyx*.

The *petals* of the flower are found under the sepals. Collectively they are known as the *corolla*, and this is the most conspicuous part of the flower. It's quite common to find little petals, or *petaloids*, between the sepals and the corolla proper.

Eight thread-like structures called *stamens* hang down from the centre of the flower, usually reaching below the corolla. Each stamen consists of a fine, hair-like section called the *filament* tipped with a tiny sac called the *anther* containing grains of *pollen*. Occasionally petaloids will form on the end of the filament. Inside the stamens is another thread-like structure, the *style*. It's usually a little longer than the stamens (though it can be shorter) and swells at its tip into the *stigma*. Together the style and the stigma form the *pistil*, the female part of the flower.

When pollen is transferred from the anther to the stigma it fertilises the flower and produces seed. Insects are attracted by a sweet-tasting *nectar* secreted at the base of the tube. As they move from flower to flower they carry pollen grains with them, nature's way of ensuring that the life-cycle continues.

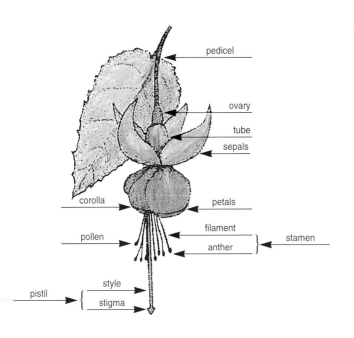

pedicel

ovary

tube

sepals

corolla

petals

filament

pollen

anther

stamen

pistil

style

stigma

9

A wealth of species

In all there are some 102 different species of the genus *Fuchsia*. The genus is divided into ten recognised sections, as follows:

Ellobium	3 species
Encliandra	6 species
Fuchsia	61 species
Hemsleyella	14 species
Jimenezia	1 species
Kierschlegeria	1 species
Pachyrrhiza	1 species
Quelusia	5 species
Schufia	2 species
Skinnera	4 species

Most of these species are found in South and Central America between the Magellan Strait and the northern boundary of Mexico, a range of some 6,000 miles (9,500 km). Others are native to some islands of the West Indies, and to Haiti, New Zealand and Tahiti.

As a result, fuchsias thrive in many different climates, ranging from cool, damp conditions in the southernmost part of their range to tropical forests and the cool slopes of the high Andes. They can be creeping, prostrate plants a few inches high or trees 30-40 ft (9-12 m) high (*F. procumbens* and *F. excorticata* , both native to New Zealand). Some species are epiphytic, and *F. fulgens* from Mexico has tuberous roots like a dahlia.

But the vast majority of species, especially those in the *Fuchsia* section, are found on the slopes of the Western Andes at heights between 5,000 and 10,000 ft (1,500 m-3,000 m). A

few grow even higher. At this altitude the Andes are girdled by an almost perpetual belt of mist, known to Chileans as the 'eyebrow of the mountain'. The plants grow in almost constant, moisture-laden cloud, hidden within dense evergreen forests where they see little of the sun. Mean temperatures are around 55°F (13°C) and rainfall is in excess of 200 in (500 cm).

Fuchsia species are found in many countries. New Zealand has *F. perscandens* and *F. colensoi* in addition to *F. procumbens* and *F. excorticata*: all have blue pollen. *F. cyrtandroides* is native to Tahiti. *F. coccinea* occurs in Brazil in addition to *F. regia*, while *F. venusta* originates in Columbia. *F. denticulata*, erroneously called *F. serratifolia*, grows in Peru and Bolivia at heights

Above: F. denticulata

Left: F. arborescens

Right: F. boliviana

Species

F. arborescens	single	rose/red/lavender	lilac-like clusters
F. boliviana	single	red terminal	very long and narrow
F. denticulata	single	reddish pink/red	strong and upright
F. fulgens	single	bright vermilion	beautiful and pendulous
F. perscandens	single	yellow/blue and brown	curious, with blue pollen
F. procumbens	single	yellow and brown, small	blue pollen, hardy
F. sanctae-rosae	single	red/orange scarlet	very beautiful
F. splendens	single	scarlet/greenish yellow	axillary flowers

Left: F. sanctae-rosae

Right: F. fulgens *var.* gesneriana

around 10,000 ft (3,000 m). *F. boliviana* (as the name suggests) occurs in Bolivia. From Mexico and Guatemala come a splendid range of species that include *F. fulgens*, *F. splendens* and *F. arborescens*. The southern range includes *F. magellanica*, found in all its varied forms from Port Famine to Valparaiso.

Some species, in particular *F. magellanica*, have even become naturalised on the west coasts of Britain and Ireland. In general, though, the fuchsia is seen as an interloper, not native to Britain.

Most of the modern cultivars are very largely descended from *F. fulgens* and *F. magellanica* with some incursions from *F. denticulata* and *F. boliviana*. As a result the plants must be grown under somewhat artificial conditions, usually in pots or containers, and the environment must be frost-free. Fuchsias appreciate plenty of moisture and shade, and a warm, humid atmosphere.

F. tillettiana

11

Selected varieties and cultivars

List of outstanding cultivars

Choosing the best cultivars from the many thousands now available is no easy task. You may prefer the large exotic, double blooms; alternatively you may prefer the small singles, which flower more prolifically. Growth habits vary, so the lists are arranged according to different ways of training the plants.

'Swingtime'

Baskets (half)

Cultivar	Blooms	Colour	Remarks
'Autumnale'	single	gold and copper foliage	red and purple flowers
'Blanche Regina'	double	white and amethyst-violet	bold, lively flowers
'Blush of Dawn'	double	waxy white/silver-grey/lavender	pastel-shaded
'Coachman'	single	pale salmon/rich orange	one of the best in its class
'Falling Stars'	single	pale scarlet/turkey red	very striking colour
'Jack Shahan'	single	rose/bengal rose	vigorous, excellent
'La Campanella'	semi-double	white/pink/purple	small flower, very free-flowering
'Mrs W. Rundle'	single	flesh-pink/orange vermilion	long, exotic flowers
'Pink Marshmallow'	double	pink/white and pink	very large blooms
'Princessita'	single	white/deep rose	plenty of small flowers
'Swingtime'	double	rich red/sparkling white	outstanding trailer
'Walsingham'	semi-double	white/rose-pink/pale lilac	beautiful and exotic

Above: *'Fiery Spider'*

'Pink Galore'

Baskets (full)

Cultivar	Blooms	Colour	Remarks
'Crackerjack'	single	white–pink/pale blue	lantern-like flowers
'Daisy Bell'	single	pale orange/vermilion orange	masses of small flowers
'Dusky Rose'	double	deep pink/deep coral pink	vigorous and good
'Fiery Spider'	single	pale salmon/crimson orange	unusual, lantern-like flowers
'Golden Marinka'	single	rich red/red	beautiful foliage
'Harry Gray'	double	white with faint rose-pink	one of the very best
'Jack Acland'	single	rose/bengal rose	good, very vigorous
'La Campanella'	semi-double	white/pink/purple	outstanding
'Lakeside'	single	reddish pink/blue–violet	exceptionally floriferous
'Lena'	semi-double	pale pink/rosy magenta	versatile and good
'Marinka'	single	rich red/red	outstanding basket
'Pink Galore'	double	pink/candy pink	almost a pink self
'Swingtime'	double	rich red/sparkling white	outstanding and large
'Trail Blazer'	double	pale magenta/dark magenta	a double 'red spider'
'Walsingham'	semi-double	white/rose-pink/pale lilac	beautiful pastel shades

Bush and shrub

Cultivar	Blooms	Colour	Remarks
'Ann H.Tripp'	single	white pink/white	one of the best whites
'Annabel'	double	white/white and pink	large and free
'Beacon'	single	deep pink/mauvish pink	hardy, 2 ft (60 cm) high
'Billy Green'	single	pinkish salmon self	triphylla type
'Bon Accorde'	single	waxy white/pale purple	erect, delicate flowers
'Border Queen'	single	rhodamine pink/violet/pink	bell-shaped flower
'Cambridge Louie'	single	pink–orange/rosy pink	extremely floriferous
'Celia Smedley'	single	neyron rose/currant red	very vigorous
'Cloverdale Pearl'	single	white–pink/white	very floriferous
'Countess of Aberdeen'	single	white flushed with pale pink	delightful near white
'Dusky Beauty'	single	neyron rose/purple and pink	floriferous and good
'Heidi Ann'	double	crimson/lilac and cerise	wins at all shows
'Lady Isobel Barnett'	single	rosy red/rose–purple	very prolific
'Margaret Roe'	single	red/pale violet	showbench banker
'Mieke Meursing'	single	red and pink	very free flowering
'Nellie Nuttall'	single	red and white	erect flowering
'Pacquesa'	single	red and white	bell-shaped flowers
'Pink Darling'	single	dark pink/soft lilac pink	lovely, almost a self
'Shellford'	single	baby pink/white	exhibitor's banker
'Snowcap'	semi-double	red/white-veined cerise	never off the showbench
'Tom Thumb'	single	carmine and mauve	small but excellent
'Westminster Chimes'	semi-double	rose and violet–blue	raiser's best introduction.
'White Joy'	single	white flushed with pink	very upright and free

Left: *'Shellford'*

Right: *'Snowcap' at home — otherwise never off the exhibition showbench*

Above: *'Border Queen' is very free-flowering.*

'Jack Shahan', with its vigorous, lax growth, is also very good for half- or full-basket cultivation.

Conicals, espaliers, pillars and pyramids

Cultivar	Blooms	Colour	Remarks
'Barbara'	single	pink/tangerine pink	extremely vigorous
'Border Queen'	single	rhodamine pink/violet/pink	very free flowering
'Coachman'	single	pale salmon/orange vermilion	one of the best oranges
'Constance'	double	pale pink/mauve pink	hardy, vigorous
'Display'	single	almost a pink self	bell-shaped flowers
'Herald'	single	scarlet and deep purple	old, but still on showbenches
'Jack Shahan'	single	rose/rose bengal	vigorous, very good
'Joan Smith'	single	flesh-pink/pink/cerise	the fastest and tallest
'Lena'	semi-double	pale pink/rosy magenta	versatile with no faults
'Mrs Lovell Swisher'	single	pinkish white/deep rose	continuous flowers
'Muriel'	semi-double	scarlet and light purple	nearly as fast as 'Joan Smith'
'Snowcap'	semi-double	red/white-veined cerise	another showbench winner
'Swingtime'	double	rich red/sparkling white	no collection should be without this
'White Spider'	single	baby pink/whitish pink	nearly an 'all white'

Floriferous

Cultivar	Blooms	Colour	Remarks
'Border Queen'	single	rhodamine pink/violet/pink	exhibitor's banker
'Cambridge Louie'	single	pink orange/rosy pink	extremely vigorous
'Lady Isobel Barnett'	single	rosy red/rose purple	probably the most floriferous
'Mieke Meursing'	single	red and pink	very good, but flowers dull
'Plenty'	single	carmine/violet purple	bell-shaped, floriferous
'Snowcap'	semi-double	red/white-veined cerise	old established, good
'Westminster Chimes'	semi-double	rose and violet–blue	bright colouring

'Snowcap'

'Walsingham'

Pastel-shaded

Cultivar	Blooms	Colour	Remarks
'Blush of Dawn'	double	waxy white/silver-grey/lavender	exotic and beautiful
'Cliff's Own'	single	waxy white/hyacinth blue	lovely contrast
'Cliff's Unique'	double	light pink/light violet-pink	delightful in every way
'Shady Blue'	single	carmine rose/pale peach	delicate and lovely
'Shy Lady'	double	creamy ivory/pale peach	has to be seen
'Walsingham'	semi-double	white/rose-pink/pale lilac	exotic and wonderful

Standards (miniature)

Cultivar	Blooms	Colour	Remarks
'Christmas Elf'	single	bright red/white and red	small flowers
'Cloverdale Jewel'	semi-double	neyron rose/wisteria blue	aptly named, lovely
'Countess of Aberdeen'	single	white flushed with pale pink	cannot be faulted
'Curly Q'	single	whitish carmine/violet-blue	quaint and neat
'Derby Imp'	single	crimson/violet-blue	small but excellent
'Joan's Delight'	single	crimson/rich violet-blue	one of the best in its class
'Little Beauty'	single	flesh-pink and lavender blue	the name says everything
'Minirose'	single	pale rose/dark rose	very vigorous and upright
'Papoose'	semi-double	red and purple	always in flower
'Ravensbarrow'	single	scarlet and purple	correct flowers for miniature
'Son of Thumb'	single	cerise and lilac	creates attention
'Tom Thumb'	single	carmine and mauve	old but outstanding
'Westminster Chimes'	semi-double	rose and violet-blue	bold, bright colours

'Derby Imp' **(left)**, *'Westminster Chimes'* **(above)** and *'Minirose'* **(below)** all make good miniature standards.

17

Standards (quarter or half)

Cultivar	Blooms	Colour	Remarks
'Bon Accorde'	single	waxy white/pale pink	erect flowers
'Chang'	single	orange red/brilliant orange	best outside
'China Lantern'	single	deep pink/white/rosy pink	continuous flowers
'Countess of Aberdeen'	single	white flushed with pale pink	good in all respects
'Lady Thumb'	single	red and white	red and white of the 'Thumbs'
'Lindisfarne'	semi-double	pale pink/dark violet	very upright, vigorous
'Lye's Unique'	single	waxy white/salmon orange	cannot be faulted
'Margaret Roe'	single	rose red and pale violet	exhibitor's banker
'Micky Goult'	single	white and violet–blue	plenty of small blooms
'Pee Wee Rose'	single	rosy red and rose	hardy up to 3 ft (90 cm)
'Son of Thumb'	single	cerise and lilac	small but good
'Tom Thumb'	single	carmine and mauve	very small, vigorous
'White Joy'	single	white flushed with pink	good 'white'

'Lindisfarne' — vigorous and very upright

'Micky Goult'

SPECIES AND VARIETIES

Standards (full)

Cultivar	Blooms	Colour	Remarks
'Achievement'	single	red and purple	good old cultivar
'Barbara'	single	pink/tangerine pink	extremely vigorous
'Celia Smedley'	single	neyron rose/currant red	excellent in its class
'Cloverdale Pearl'	single	white pink/white	nearly a 'white'
'Display'	single	almost a pink self	versatile, very good
'Dollar Princess'	double	cerise/rich purple	proved over a long time
'Flirtation Waltz'	double	creamy white/pink/shell pink	beautiful, bruises easily
'Lady Isobel Barnett'	single	rosy red/rose purple	very floriferous
Lye's cultivars (any)		creamy waxy tube and sepals	all very good
'Mieke Meursing'	single	red and pink	extremely floriferous
'Mrs Lovell Swisher'	single	pinkish white/deep old rose	flowers vigorously
'Nancy Lou'	double	deep clear pink/brilliant white	beautiful
'Other Fellow'	single	waxy white and coral pink	good American
'Pink Darling'	single	dark pink and soft lilac pink	lovely, the best of the pinks
'Shady Blue'	single	carmine rose/blue violet	pastel-shaded, lovely
'Snowcap'	semi-double	red/white-veined cerise	cannot be left out

Left: *'Celia Smedley'*

Below: *'Barbara' as a three-year standard*

19

SPECIES AND VARIETIES

Whites

Cultivar	Blooms	Colour	Remarks
'Ann H. Tripp'	single	white pink/white	well shaped flower
'Annabel'	double	white/white and pink	delightful
'Bobby Shaftoe'	semi-double	frosty white/pale pink	unique frosty colour
'Countess of Aberdeen'	single	white flushed with pale pink	beautiful colouring
'Flying Cloud'	double	white with faintest of pink	the first 'all white'
'Frank Unsworth'	double	white with slight pink flush	good double
'Harry Gray'	double	white with faint rose-pink	best in class
'Roy Walker'	double	white with tinge of pink	bold and vigorous
'Ting-a-Ling'	single	all-white self	as near white as possible
'White Joy'	single	white flushed with pink	vigorous and good

Left: *'Roy Walker'*

Right: *'Annabel'*

Cultivars with British Fuchsia Society awards
First-class certificate

Cultivar	Blooms	Colour	Remarks
'Annabel'	double	white/white and pink	large blooms, very good
'Billy Green'	single	pinkish salmon self	triphylla type
'Border Queen'	single	rhodamine pink/violet pink	always with winning card
'Celia Smedley'	single	neyron rose/currant red	outstanding cultivar
'Display'	single	almost a pink self	old, but hardly a fault
'Joy Patmore'	single	waxy white/rich carmine	colouring cannot be bettered
'Marinka'	single	rich red/red	'the' basket cultivar
'Royal Velvet'	double	crimson red/deep purple	large, imposing flowers
'Snowcap'	semi-double	red/white-veined cerise	old, but always winning
'Swingtime'	double	rich red/sparkling white	one of the best trailers

'Billy Green' (**below**) and 'Joy Patmore' (**right**) have both won first-class certificates.

21

Above: *'Thalia', an attractive triphylla, has won an Award of merit.*

Left: *'Alison Ewart'* — highly commended

Cultivars with British Fuchsia Society awards
Award of merit

Cultivar	Blooms	Colour	Remarks
'Citation'	single	red and white	very flat bell-shaped
'Cloverdale Pearl'	single	white pink/white	exhibitor's banker
'Eva Boerg'	semi-double	pale pink/rosy magenta	versatile, superb
'Genii'	single	violet/cerise	golden foliage, long
'Heidi Ann'	double	crimson/lilac and cerise	prizewinner at all shows
'La Campanella'	semi-double	white/pink/purple	excellent basket cultivar
'Mieke Meursing'	single	red and white	dull flowers but floriferous
'Mrs Popple'	single	scarlet/purple violet	one of the best hardies
'Nellie Nuttall'	single	red and white	another for the showbench
'Pacquesa'	single	red and white	bell-shaped and shapely
'Tennessee Waltz'	double	rose madder/lilac–lavender	good American
'Thalia'	single	rich orange–scarlet	very long tubes
'Tom Thumb'	single	carmine/mauve	old, still very popular

Highly commended

Cultivar	Blooms	Colour	Remarks
'Alison Ewart'	single	neyron rose/mauve-pink	small flowers, attractive
'Checkerboard'	single	red/white/red	unusual, changes colours
'Flirtation Waltz'	double	creamy white/pink/shell pink	exquisite flowers, but they bruise
'Lady Isobel Barnett'	single	rosy red/rose purple	extremely floriferous
'Leonora'	single	pale pink self	bell-shaped flowers
'Margaret Roe'	single	rosy red and pale violet	exhibitor's banker
'Martin Glow'	single	waxy white/imperial purple	cannot be beaten for colour

Triphyllas — a gift from the rain forest

The word *triphylla* means three-leaved, from the Greek *tri* (three) and *phyllon* (a leaf). Triphyllas look different from other fuchsias because their leaves are grouped in threes rather than twos.

These hybrids of the first known species, *F. triphylla*, are among the most beautiful of fuchsias. Most are the result of crosses between the species *F. triphylla*, *F. fulgens*, *F. corymbiflora* or *F. splendens*. As all the parents come from a subtropical habitat, triphyllas need a little more attention than most fuchsias. They are particularly frost-shy, and need to be kept under glass while they are overwintering. During the winter make sure they aren't exposed to temperatures below 40°F (4°C).

The leaves of triphyllas are very attractive, usually dark green with coloured veins. The flowers, carried in terminal clusters, are different, too. The characteristic long tube, and the small corolla and petals, make them look like a symmetrical four-pointed star (a few have six rather than four points). All flower vigorously, and will bloom in winter as long as they get enough light and heat.

Triphyllas prefer a loam-based compost, and flower better in conventional clay pots. It's best not to *stop* them (i.e. nip off the growing tip — see page 73) too often: twice or three times is enough. The plants will benefit from a longer period of growth (which could be as much as fourteen weeks) after the final stop.

Unfortunately all triphyllas, especially the original species, tend to shed their lower leaves, and without warmth and humidity the flowers will often drop prematurely.

Growth is usually upright and bushy, which makes them ideal for bedding out as half-hardies. 'Thalia' and 'Gartenmeister Bonstedt' are probably best for this, but most triphyllas will stand more sun than other fuchsias, making good bush plants of considerable size. 'Billy Green', 'Coralle' and 'Gartenmeister Bonstedt' grow more vigorously, so they can be trained as half or quarter standards (see page 32). 'Mantilla' and 'Trumpeter' are an excellent choice for baskets.

All are easy to obtain from nurserymen who specialise in fuchsias.

'Our Ted'

The most popular triphyllas

Cultivar	Date	Colour	Habit
'Billy Green'	Unknown 1966	pinkish salmon self	upright
'Coralle'	Bonstedt 1905	salmon–orange self	upright
'Gartenmeister Bonstedt'	Bonstedt 1905	orange/brick red self	upright
'Leverkusen'	Rehnelt 1928	rosy cerise self	upright
'Mantilla'	Reiter 1945	deep carmine	trailing
'Mary'	Bonstedt 1894	vivid bright scarlet self	upright
'Thalia'	Bonstedt 1905	rich orange–scarlet self	upright
'Trumpeter'	Reiter 1946	pale geranium–lake self	trailer

Ornamental and variegated cultivars

There is no official definition of an 'ornamental' cultivar, or one with 'variegated foliage'. Even so, most people would describe ornamental cultivars as those grown for the beauty of their leaves. Their foliage is distinctly yellow (usually golden yellow), and sometimes has a red blush, or an overlay of a second colour (e.g. 'Golden Treasure' and 'Cloth of Gold').

Fuchsias with variegated foliage have two or more distinct leaf colours. 'Autumnale' is typical, with golden and coppery-red leaves changing to dark red, salmon, mahogany and russet. 'Golden Marinka' has cream edges and patches on a yellow or green leaf. Red-veined foliage is not recognised as ornamental or variegated unless it has some other distinct characteristic.

Most cultivars are not free-flowering. Red and purple is the most usual colouring, but exposure (or lack of exposure) to sunlight can cause the colours to vary. Cultivars are very sensitive to light. They will tolerate full sunlight, but if they are heavily shaded you will find that their colour will be greatly reduced.

Feeding can also produce different results: use fertiliser with a high nitrogen content in preference to a potassium feed.

Take care when spraying and watering; careless application could badly mark or even spoil the leaves. All these cultivars prefer their compost on the dry side; overwatering causes leaf drop, so the compost should be almost dry before you water the plant.

'Tom West' — an excellent example of a variegated cultivar

24

The aubergines — a breakthrough in colour

In recent years Dutch and German hybridists have achieved a remarkable breakthrough in colour by crossing hitherto unused species. The aubergine (eggplant) colour of these cultivars is completely new; the nearest natural equivalent is that of the New Zealand species *F. excorticata* and *F. perscandens*. The very first attempts to introduce this new colour were made in Britain in 1980 when John Wright, then of Reading and Lechlade, crossed *F. excorticata* with *F. magellanica* to produce his 'Whiteknight's Amethyst'. This magellanican flower type has an exotic red–purple tube and sepals, and a vivid violet corolla. In 1985 the Dutchman, Herman de Graaff, started his long list of aubergines with 'Highland Pipes' and two of his most exciting creations, 'Purple Rain' and 'Zulu Queen'. Herman has now obtained large-flowered double aubergines among his seedlings by using *F. lycioides*.

Perhaps the most popular and exciting aubergines are 'Foolke' and 'Foline' from Lutz Bogemann of Germany, available from many specialist nurseries.

*The subtle coloration of an aubergine cultivar is very difficult to capture on film — 'Foline' (**below left**) and 'Purple Rain' (**below**).*

The most popular aubergine cultivars

Cultivar	Dominant parent	Colour	Habit
'Foline'	*F. excorticata*	purple/reddish purple	upright
'Foolke'	*F. excorticata*	magenta/dark plum	upright
'Fuchsiade 88'	*F. excorticata*	reddish purple/dark purple	upright
'Haute Cuisine'	'Zulu Queen'	magenta/reddish purple	trailer
'Highland Pipes'	*F. excorticata*	beetroot purple/ruby red	lax
'Purple Rain'	*F. excorticata*	reddish purple/dark purple	upright
'Zulu Queen'	*F. excorticata*	dark cardinal red/cardinal red	upright

Biennial cultivation

There are many ways to grow fuchsias. *Current growth* cultivation means that the plant is allowed to grow and flower in its first year. *Normal growth* cultivation involves pruning and repotting the plants in late winter or early spring. But the *biennial* method is by far the best. Most top exhibitors use it to produce their show specimens, especially those that will be trained as shrubs.

'Dusky Beauty'

Biennial plants complete their flowering in their second year. You will need to start by taking cuttings in early summer, preferably in May or June. At this time you can be sure of getting choice material either from stock plants or from young plants. Young plants are better, especially if you can get three-leaved shoots.

When the cuttings have rooted (normally after 14–18 days), pot them up individually into 2 in (5 cm) or 2¼ in (5.5 cm) pots, using good soilless compost (my choice would be Humber compost). They won't need any additional heat at this time of year, so you can leave them to grow perfectly naturally. As the plants grow they will need to be transferred to larger pots (*potted on*). Use a pot 1 in (2.5 cm) bigger than its predecessor, potting on whenever the plant requires it. Meanwhile stop them and feed them in the normal way.

I prefer to make the young plant as hard as possible. Standing it out in the open, or in a cold frame, during the summer ensures a strong and sturdy basis for the second year's growth. The plant is not allowed to flower; you can prevent this by regular stopping.

By September or October the plant will be growing in a 4 in (10 cm) or 5 in (13 cm) pot. (Don't use anything larger.) At

this point you can encourage it to enter a semi-dormant state by gradually withdrawing its water and food. You are aiming for growth that is just 'ticking over' through November, December and January. Unfortunately, this comes at a price. You must ensure a minimum temperature of 40°F (4°C) and a maximum of 45°F (7°C), *day and night*, to keep the plant in green leaf. Don't allow it to shed all its leaves, though some of them are bound to fall. Water carefully to obtain the ideal soil condition; it should be slightly damp. The plant is really 'in limbo'. It isn't dormant, nor is it entirely active; perhaps it can best be described as 'resting'.

As the light starts to improve towards the end of January and into February, the plants will begin to look completely different. Now they are ready to be *potted back*. This involves removing part of the root ball and soil, and then replacing the plant in a smaller pot. Those in 5 in (13 cm) pots should be returned to 4 in (10 cm) pots. Those in 4 in (10 cm) pots should be potted back to 3 in (7.5 cm) or 3¼ in (8.25 cm) pots. The biennial plants will have plenty of new, white roots (very different from the old, brown roots of normal overwintered plants), so handle them carefully. Make sure the new roots aren't lost or damaged when you're repotting, and do be certain that any soil you use is new and fresh. Some growers prefer to pot on in January or

No flowers yet — this 'White Joy' specimen is being grown using the biennial method.

February, but in my experience potting back produces better results.

After repotting (or potting on) treat the plants in the normal way, potting on an inch at a time when the roots have worked nicely around the root ball. You can resume normal feeding as soon as the plants have recovered from any check. Use a feed with high nitrogen content; a 3-1-1 ratio should be ideal (see page 63). Stopping should be done as for other methods of training: allow 8–10 weeks for singles and 10–12 weeks for doubles, stopping after every two pairs of leaves (though most successful exhibitors stop after one pair of

leaves, especially with shrub and bush shapes — see also page 30).

The biennial method is ideal for training standards, baskets, and indeed most shapes, especially bushes and shrubs. Short-jointed cultivars such as 'Tom Thumb', 'Countess of Aberdeen', 'Heidi Ann', 'Lena Dalton', 'Mieke Meursing', 'Plenty', 'Lady Isobel Barnett' and 'Pink Darling' are admirably suited to this method, and stopping them hard produces huge, tight heads.

27

What's the point of training fuchsias?

Below: *These fuchsias are being trained as bonsai.*

The fuchsia is probably the most adaptable of all shrubs, and can be trained to all recognised shapes. In their natural habitat fuchsia species are very diverse, producing anything from creeping, prostrate plants to very high trees. As a result we have to grow them artificially — and that's why we need to train them. All upright, vigorous fuchsia cultivars make good bushes, and can also be trained into taller forms such as standards, conicals and pillars. Most of the Californian introductions have a lax habit that makes them ideal for baskets or for weeping standards.

Below: *'Impudence' on a trellis*

A greenhouse full of fuchsias can be a riot of colour in August.

Below: *'Belsay Beauty'*

Bush training

The bush shape is the most popular and the easiest to produce, which makes it ideal for the beginner. Even so, it doesn't just happen. You'll have to work to produce the proper shape, though a few natural, self-branching cultivars will make plants of the right shape with a single stopping.

You will need to start with a fairly vigorous cultivar raised from a cutting. Don't begin *any* training before both the roots and the top of the cutting have made good growth. This will usually be during the first or second potting-on stage, when the cutting is in a 2½ in (6.5 cm) or 3½ in (9 cm) pot. When the plant has developed three pairs of leaves, remove the central growing tip; this is the first stop or *pinch* (see page 73), and it will encourage side shoots to develop in the axils. When these shoots have produced two pairs of leaves, they too are stopped. This will generate six shoots from the original central shoot. All these shoots will break again, and again the tips are pinched when each shoot has produced two further pairs of leaves. As a result of this second stop you'll now have twenty-four shoots. For normal decorative training this is perfectly adequate, but growers who need large specimens can continue stopping until they're satisfied. Remember that all stoppings should be made at the same time, and that each stopping will delay flowering by several weeks.

Exhibitors on the showbench favour a very tight head. You can achieve this by pinching out at one pair of leaves.

A plant that is being trained needs good compost, and it should be encouraged to grow by moving it routinely into a larger pot. Start with a 3½ in (9 cm) pot, then use a 4¼ in (11 cm) and then a 5 in (13 cm) pot.

On current growth (i.e. with first-year plants) the 5 in (13 cm) pot is large enough, but with very vigorous cultivars and old established plants the final pot could be as large as 6 in (15 cm). You must protect the plants from excessive sunlight at each stage of potting on to stop them wilting. After watering, put them in the shadiest part of the greenhouse to recover from the check to their growth. An ideal place is under the staging.

Well-grown bush plants should be symmetrical, with even growth on all sides. You can achieve this by giving the plant a half-turn every third day, which prevents one-sided flowering. Grow the plants as hard as possible: this will prevent soft growth (which may not carry the weight of the flowers) and avoids the need for excessive staking. They will be much stronger and healthier if

'White Joy'

they are left out in the open during the summer, in the shadiest position. When you're arranging fuchsias (especially on staging) never let the leaves of one plant overlap those of another. This will help to prevent long shoots and weak, 'over-drawn' growth (i.e. excessively elongated).

Training a plant as a bush, showing the first and second stops

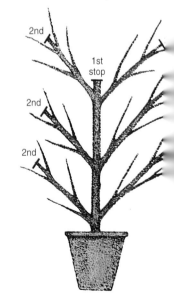

'Waveney Sunrise'

Cultivars suitable for bush training

Cultivar	Date	Bloom	Colours
'Annabel'	Ryle 1977	double	white flushed with pink
'Beacon'	Bull 1871	single	deep pink/mauvish pink
'Bon Accorde'	Crousse 1861	single	waxy white/pale purple
'Border Queen'	Ryle 1974	single	rhodamine pink/pale pink
'Cloverdale Pearl'	Gadsby 1974	single	white flushed with pink
'Countess of Aberdeen'	Cocker 1888	single	white flushed with pale pink
'Heidi Ann'	Smith 1969	double	crimson/bright lilac
'Margaret Roe'	Gadsby 1968	single	red/pale violet
'Mieke Meursing'	Hopwood 1968	single	red/pink
'Nellie Nuttall'	Roe 1977	single	red/white
'Pacquesa'	Clyne 1974	semi-double	deep red/white
'Pink Darling'	Machado 1961	single	dark pink/soft lilac pink
'Snowcap'	Henderson 1880	semi-double	red/white and cerise
'Tom Thumb'	Baudinat 1850	single	carmine/mauve
'Westminster Chimes'	Clyne 1976	semi-double	rose/violet–blue
'White Joy'	Burns 1980	single	white flushed with pink

Standards

After training a bush, most enthusiasts try to train a standard. Standards are best described as bush plants growing on a clear stem of a certain length. Different lengths of stem will produce full, half, quarter and miniature standards. You don't have to follow the measurements given in the table on page 34, but they do produce a balanced, well-regulated plant.

Take an early cutting from a strong, upright cultivar such as 'Snowcap'. This cultivar is one of a small number that will often throw three sets of leaves rather than the usual two, which produces an even better standard. Grow the cutting unchecked (i.e. without stopping it). When the time comes to pot on, it will have made enough growth to need some support. Insert a cane fairly close to the stem, and tie the plant to it fairly loosely at intervals of 2–3 in (5–7.5 cm). Keep the plant tied up throughout the training period: this ensures a straight stem. While the plant is gaining height and making rapid new growth, be sure to keep turning it so it remains symmetrical. All plants will grow towards the strongest light source, especially if they are under glass.

The next stage is important, too. While the plant is gaining height you should remove all the side shoots that appear in

the leaf axils, apart from the topmost two or three. Eventually these will form the head. Don't remove any of the leaves on the stem until the standard is finished: the plant will need them to feed and to breathe.

From here on you are aiming for rapid, unchecked growth, and you can achieve it by potting on regularly. Use a pot that is 1 in (2.5 cm) larger than its predecessor. Pay close attention to the condition of the roots; as soon as you can see a definite root system all around the ball of soil, the plant should

Above: *A plant being trained as a mini-standard: note where the side-shoots have been removed.*

Three stages in training a standard

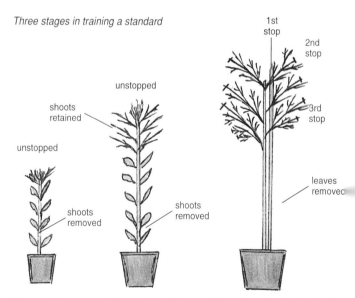

Young plant unstopped — side shoots removed but leaves retained

Young whip with shoots retained at the top

Plant stopped when desired height reached — top three shoots form head after stopping

'Phyllis' trained as a standard

miniature, and full standards may need more). Treat these in exactly the same way as the bush plant, stopping them each time they have produced two pairs of leaves. Usually three or four stops will be enough to produce a well-balanced head. If you want a very tight head, you could begin in the normal way by stopping after the first two pairs of leaves, then stop after each single pair.

The head of your finished standard should be about one-third of the total height of the plant; its width should be about two-thirds of the total height. In winter, established standards need slightly higher temperatures, around 38°F (3°C), when they are resting: tall plants are

Below: *'Celia Smedley' makes a really excellent standard.*

be potted on. If the young *whip* (as it is now known) becomes potbound it will probably bud, or even flower. Neither is desirable while you are trying to produce more height. In either case practically all the plant's upward growth will come to a halt, and removing the bud or flower will effectively act as a topping.

Don't overlook feeding. Nitrogen fertiliser applied during the training period will help to promote rapid growth. Always increase the length of the cane

or support some inches above the height that the plant has achieved. As it approaches its target height, make sure there are at least three pairs of leaves at the top. Grow the plant on until these leaf pairs are above the intended height of the clear stem: they will form the head of the finished standard.

At this point it's time for a stop, so you should remove the leading (or central) shoot. Ideally there should be four side shoots left in the head (though three may be enough for a

Suitable cultivars for standards

Cultivar	Colour	Remarks
'Barbara'	pink/tangerine pink	full or half standard
'Brenda White'	carmine/white	dainty, excellent miniature
'Celia Smedley'	neyron rose/currant red	very vigorous for full standard
'Derby Imp'	crimson/violet-blue	miniature
'Display'	almost a dark pink self	full or half standard
'Dusky Beauty'	neyron rose/pinkish purple	miniature, very easy
'Lena'	pale pink/rosy magenta	versatile, very easy
'Little Beauty'	red/purple	miniature, outstanding
'Pink Darling'	almost a pale pink self	full, very dependable
'Snowcap'	red/white	a must for full standard
'Tom Thumb'	red/purple	miniature

generally more vulnerable to frost. Prune them in the early spring, cutting them back harder than the normal bush plant.

The table opposite lists the British Fuchsia Society's recommendations for the length of clear stem from soil level to the lowest branch of the standard.

BFS recommendations for length of clear stem

Miniature	not less than 6 in (15 cm)	nor exceeding 10 in (25 cm)
Quarter	not less than 10 in (25 cm)	nor exceeding 18 in (45 cm)
Half	not less than 18 in (45 cm)	nor exceeding 30 in (75 cm)
Full	not less than 30 in (75 cm)	nor exceeding 42 in (105 cm)

'Angel's Dream'

Basket cultivation

There's no doubt that well-grown baskets are both spectacular and eye-catching. For the best results the plant growth should fill the centre and top of the basket, surging over the edge in a sweeping cascade. You should aim for uniform growth, with an abundance of flowers that effectively conceal the basket.

Baskets should be planted during March, or by early April at the latest. This ensures a long period of growth, which is just what you need to produce healthy, trailing, flowering laterals. In my experience current growth is the best way to produce good results, so empty your baskets every year and start again with new plants.

Baskets come in a variety of sizes from 10 to 15 in (25–38 cm), and a choice of materials. I prefer the older galvanised-wire baskets to the modern plastic-covered types. It's probably better to plant a single cultivar rather than mixing, since this makes it easier to maintain growth, balance, and continuous flowering. A 10 in (25 cm) basket can hold three plants, a 12 in (30 cm) basket can hold four, and a 15 in (38 cm) basket will hold five or six. For the best results, use plants produced from autumn cuttings. If these

are not available, choose plants from very early struck cuttings, or buy them from specialist nurseries. Ideally they should be in 3¼ in (8.25 cm) pots.

Baskets have round bases, so don't try to fill them on a flat surface. It's far easier to deal with them if they're supported in a bucket or a large flower pot. Line the basket with green moss (if you can get it), or with a sheet of polythene, pierced with several small holes at the base to ensure proper drainage. Put a fair quantity of peat at the bottom of the basket and then fill it almost to the top with a good soilless compost.

Planting calls for a little care. The plants shouldn't be vertical; it's better to plant them round the edge of the basket at an angle of 45°, which ensures they're already trailing a little. You can put one small plant in

the middle of the basket if you wish, but in my experience it isn't necessary; the other plants will soon spread out to cover the entire area. Firm each plant into place with finger pressure only, and make a saucer-shaped depression in the compost in the middle of the basket to help retain water. Water the basket well in with a fine-rosed can, and leave it in a shady place for a few days. Be careful not to overwater at this stage: it's better to leave the basket until it has almost dried out before you water it again.

Once they have been watered, hanging baskets can become very heavy, especially when you are using a soil-based compost. Never hang them from the sash bars or the rafters of the greenhouse, unless you are sure that the structure will bear the weight.

Stop the plants when they have formed three pairs of leaves, and then pinch out at every three pairs of leaves. After

'Coachman' in a half-basket

'Swingtime' — among the most popular fuchsias for baskets

three or four pinchings you will produce long, trailing, flowering stems, but do remember that the plants will then take eight to ten weeks to flower.

Wall baskets or half baskets are now very popular, and can be planted and cultivated in exactly the same way. For 10-12 in (25-30 cm) baskets, use two plants from 3¼ in (8.25 cm) pots. For a 14 in (35 cm) basket, use three. The measurement is the longest dimension across the back of the basket.

The best cultivars for baskets

Cultivar	Date	Bloom	Colour	Remarks
'Dancing Flame'	Stubbs 1981	double	pale orange/orange carmine	exotic, beautiful flower from California
'Golden Marinka'	Weber 1955	single	scarlet/velvet red	sport of 'Marinka' with variegated foliage
'Harry Gray'	Dunnett 1975	double	white-tipped pink/ creamy white	delightful small 'powder puff' blooms
'Jack Acland'	Haag 1952	single	bright pink/rosy red	heat tolerant, good show cultivar from California
'La Campanella'	Blackwell 1968	semi-double	white flushed with pink/purple	produces an amazing number of small, semi-double blooms
'Lena'	Bunney 1862	semi-double	flesh-pink/purple and plum	very versatile, premier show basket for years
'Marinka'	Rozain 1902	single	scarlet red/velvet red	the best basket cultivar for many years
'Pink Galore'	Walker 1958	double	pink/candy pink	glossy leaves; good for wall or full basket
'Pres. Stanley Wilson'	Thorne 1968	single	carmine/rose carmine	continuous flowering of first-class quality
'Rose of Denmark'	Banks 1864	semi-double	blush pink/rose-pink	very delicate and beautiful blooms
'Swingtime'	Tiret 1950	double	cerise and white	the most popular and outstanding trailer

Hanging pots

Baskets, especially large baskets, tend to take up more space than some growers can spare, and they're difficult to move. Hanging containers — plastic pots supplied complete with three hanger stays — offer a new and welcome alternative. The popular sizes are 6 in (15 cm) and 8 in (20 cm).

It's a pity that many growers still seem to be using the wrong cultivars. Don't choose large flowering doubles or stiff, upright cultivars, and try to avoid cultivars that grow too far out from the pot. Their habit should be trailing or lax, and you are looking for small or medium-sized blooms.

Suitable choices might include 'Westminster Chimes', 'Harry Gray', 'Derby Imp', 'La Campanella', 'Border Queen',

'Christmas Elf', 'Daisy Bell', 'Lena', 'Little Jewel', 'Fiona', 'Magic Flute', 'President Stanley Wilson' and 'Walsingham'; of these, 'Westminster Chimes' is outstanding.

As regards cultivation, you can use an early spring cutting that has been potted on gradually through the 3 in (7.5 cm) and 4 in (10 cm) sizes, or even to a 5 in (13 cm) pot. Successful flowering would be possible with current growth, but I find that second-year plants produce more acceptable results.

If you are growing for personal pleasure rather than for the showbench, try taking two or even three spring cuttings from your 3 in (7.5 cm) pots and putting them straight into the hanging container for quick results. If possible, choose a self-branching cultivar that will

produce plenty of growth without too many stops.

The ideal plant will be trained as closely as possible into the shape of a ball of flowers, completely hiding the container. Try to grow the plant so it remains in proportion to the size of its container. An enormous plant in a small pot looks completely wrong, and a small plant with few laterals will not look its best in a large pot.

If you are using a second-year plant, choose one that has been pruned and repotted (potted back) in a 3 in (7.5 cm) pot by early February. Continue normal spring cultivation by potting on gradually to 4 in (10 cm) and 5 in (13 cm) pots. Stop and pinch the plant when necessary, and don't forget the initial feeding.

By May it should be ready for potting on into its final hanging pot or container. This is the time to insert the plastic hanging stays so the plant can grow around the pot and the hangers. If the plant is properly fed, you should have a riot of colour by the middle of July.

'Westminster Chimes' in a hanging pot

Fuchsias as climbers

In Britain (and, indeed, in most temperate countries) fuchsias can be grown as greenhouse or conservatory climbers by training a main stem up along the rafters. Cultivation is quite easy. Start with a strong, vigorous plant and remove all the side shoots until you achieve the height you are looking for. Then remove the top, and allow three or four pairs of shoots to develop (as you would with a standard), training them along the greenhouse rafters as required. The resulting flowers will hang down gracefully, producing an attractive display well into the autumn

Climbing fuchsias should be treated like grape vines: prune them back to the main stem every spring, and clear the bark off the stem during the winter. They can be planted in large pots or tubs, though it's better to plant them *in situ* in the greenhouse or conservatory border as a permanent fixture; this helps to protect them against winter frosts.

You can see good examples of climbers at Kew Gardens, and occasionally in other botanical gardens. California provides ideal growing conditions; many Californian cultivars are grown as climbers against trellis work, reaching heights of 6–8 ft (1.8–2.4 m).

Suitable species and cultivars for climbers

'Abinger Fayre'
F. alpestris
F. boliviana
F. corymbiflora
'Dominyana'
'Elizabeth' (Whiteman)
'Joan Smith'
'Lady Boothby'
'Muriel'
'Pride of the West'
'Regal'
F. regia
'Rose of Castile'
'Rose of Castile Improved'
'Royal Purple'
F. simplicicaulis
F. venusta

Above: F. venusta *is a good species for a climber.*

Below: *'Aphrodite' being grown as a climber*

38

Other training methods

Espaliers

Although they aren't seen very often, *espaliers* make a bold show, and well-grown specimens always draw admiring attention. The diagrams show how espaliers can be trained into *horizontal* or *fan* shapes. The training method is very different from that used for other types, since the plant will be seen only from the front. The finished specimens should offer an attractive display of fresh blooms and clean foliage. There is no restriction on size, but the plant should have balanced growth.

Unless you're growing an espalier for an exhibition or a show, it's better to grow the plant *in situ* in the greenhouse border. Most other types of training demand vigorous, upright growth, but almost any cultivar can be used for an

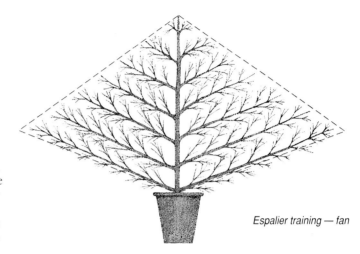

Espalier training — fan

espalier. Ideal choices are strong, lax cultivars such as 'Swingtime', 'Kathy Louise', 'Miss California', 'White Spider', 'Lena' and those two universal growers 'Fascination' and 'Mrs Lovell Swisher'.

You're aiming for a plant that has a central, upright stem, and four, five or six branches equidistant from one another along the stem. For the fan espalier the branches should be at an angle of 45° to the stem; for the horizontal espalier, they should be at right angles to it. You need to have enough laterals, and they need to be as nearly opposed to one another as possible.

Start with a plant that has been grown from the early, green tip cutting. Allow it to grow unstopped, but supported in some way at the centre. You want to achieve rapid growth by gradual potting on and feeding until the plant reaches its intended height. However, do be sure to rub out any side shoots that would upset the balance of the finished plant.

I recommend the use of a strong cane after you've potted

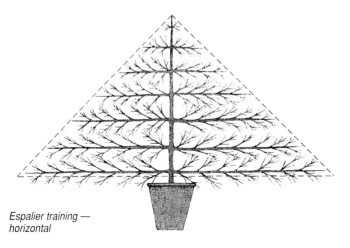

Espalier training — horizontal

on for the first or second time. Exchange this for a square stake as the plant approaches its intended height. Drill holes through this stake for the round canes that will eventually support the lateral shoots. Stop the plant when it has grown as high as necessary, and add the canes to support the laterals. From now on you can allow the side shoots to grow without any stopping until they are as long as you want them to be. As they grow, use suitable ties to fasten them onto the tops of the supports; that way later growth will conceal the framework.

Tight or close growth is essential for espalier training. To achieve it you'll need to stop all the side shoots on the laterals after one pair of leaves. The shoots resulting from this stopping are also stopped after they have made a further pair of leaves.

Right: *'Mrs Lovell Swisher'*

Below: *'Display' as an espalier*

Pillars

This type of fuchsia growing is rarely seen today, and really belongs to the Victorian and Edwardian eras. The late James Lye was a master at training this type of growth. Photographs record specimen plants several feet high and 3-4 ft (90-120 cm) across. On large estates with extensive greenhouses and experienced head gardeners, both pillars and pyramids were used to line the main path to the house, achieving effects of considerable grandeur.

With pillars, you're aiming to produce two stems, at different

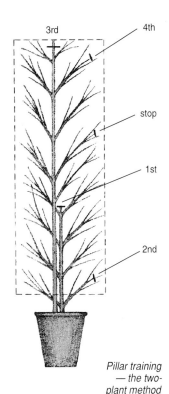

heights, with uniform growth the whole way up, and to prevent any tapering at the top.

There are two ways to do it. The first uses a single plant which is stopped after two pairs of leaves have grown. The strongest of each pair is allowed to grow; one is trained as a bush, and the other as a standard. The remaining, weaker shoots are rubbed out.

The second method uses two plants growing in the same pot; again, one is trained as a standard and the other as a bush. This is easier, and gives quicker results because it avoids the initial check to growth involved in the first stopping. Most importantly, perhaps, when growth resumes it will be more even than that of the single-plant pillar.

Choose two vigorous cuttings from cultivars such as 'Snowcap' or 'Fascination' as early as possible in the spring. Grow one as a bush, stopping it at three pairs of leaves, and the other as a standard without any stopping. At this stage both plants will probably be in their first 2 in (5 cm) or 2½ in (5.5 cm) pot. When the roots are well established, and the plants are ready to be moved into 3 in (7.5 cm) or 3¼ in (8.25 cm) pots, pot them both together. Put them side by side, with at least 1 in (2.5 cm) between the stems, into a 4 in (10 cm) or 4¼ in (11 cm) pot. At this stage you may need to shake off a little surplus soil to accommodate both plants in the new pot. Now

This 'Snowcap' pillar has been created from three plants

add a suitable cane or stick: this will be used by both plants.

If you want the pillar to reach a final height of 5 ft (1.5 m), you should aim to grow and flower the bush plant to a height of 30 in (75 cm); the standard should have a clear stem 30 in (75 cm) high and a head 30 in (75 cm) high. Keep the stems close together during their subsequent growth. Stop the bush plant at three pairs of leaves, stopping again when the resulting side shoots have made two further pairs of leaves. Make further stops as necessary to ensure all the shoots achieve

Pillar training — the two-plant method

3rd
4th
stop
1st
2nd

an even length. Meanwhile remove all side shoots from the standard until it reaches the 30 in (75 cm) mark. After this, retain all side shoots and stop them when the plant has made 5 ft (1.5 m). Continue stopping the side shoots to develop the head of the plant.

Pyramids

Training a pyramid is one of the most demanding tests of a grower's skill. Regrettably, they arc rarely seen today; like pillars, they reached their peak of popularity in the late Victori-an and early Edwardian periods. Their great exponent, James Lye, was exhibiting specimen pyramids 10 ft (3 m) high and several feet across, and his work was continued and possibly emulated by his son-in-law, G. Bright of Reading. The photographs they have left to posterity show both of them completely dwarfed by their own specimen plants.

James Lye would have taken four years to train a pyramid, but today, with constant attention and considerable patience, it can be done in two years. The plant should be at least 4 ft (1.2 m) tall from soil level to apex, and at least 3 ft (90 cm) wide at the base. Growth should be symmetrical and uniform from pot level to apex. This can only be achieved by the careful and skilful manipulation of a single stem, and you will need a strong, vigorous and upright cultivar. I suggest 'Brutus', 'Display', 'Checkerboard', any of the vigorous Lye's varieties (such as 'Amy Lye', 'Beauty of Trowbridge', 'Clipper' or 'Lye's Unique'), 'Mieke Meursing', 'Heidi Ann', 'Joy Patmore' or 'Flirtation Waltz'. Select a plant grown from an early, green tip cutting and if possible one that produces three leaves rather than the normal two. Let it grow to 9–10 in (23–25 cm) before the first stopping: this will usually leave you with three or four pairs of leaves, or between six and eight side shoots. One shoot — the one at the top that is more vigorous — is now chosen to form the new leader; the other is rubbed out. You should put a stout cane in the centre of the pot to support the main stem, all the time ensuring that it's taller than the growing leader.

From now on the plant *must* be kept growing all the time, without the slightest check. It must not bud or flower prematurely; you can prevent this with the gradual potting-on procedure described above. Regular feeding with a high-nitrogen feed will ensure rapid upward growth.

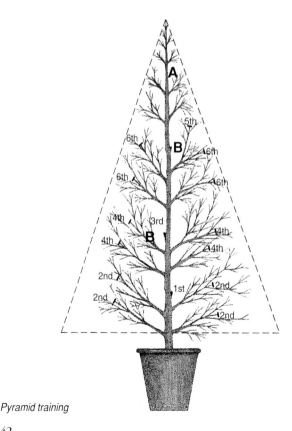

Pyramid training

This first stopping will induce the side shoots to develop. Stop these after they've produced three pairs of leaves. It's important to make all these stops at the same time, to ensure even growth. These stoppings, in turn, will produce further side shoots; these should be stopped after producing two further pairs of leaves.

By now you need to be thinking about a temporary frame-work strong enough to support the new growth from the side shoots. I recommend inserting suitable canes at an angle around the edge of the pot, and tying one or two more horizontally to the main stem, supported with green string or raffia. The side shoots can be tied to these canes.

After three or four more leaf pairs have developed on the new leader you should stop it a

A multi-pyramid of 'Ting-a-Ling'

second time. Again, take the more vigorous of the two uppermost shoots and rub out the other one. Train the remaining shoots outwards to produce your second set of horizontal laterals. Stop them after they've produced three pairs of leaves, and again after they've produced a further two pairs. Now repeat the whole process as many times as necessary to achieve the height you want.

It's essential to stop the side shoots and the leader *alternately*, and to stop all the side branches at the same time. The lowest side shoots will naturally be the longest, and in the early stages you may have to train them vertically on your temporary framework. Don't try to train them horizontally at this stage, or you will check their growth. When the buds, the flowers, and the normal-sized branches appear, these shoots

Conical training

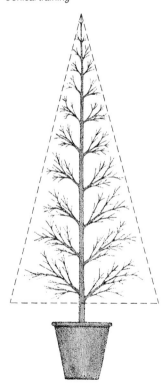

will fall into position of their own accord, in much the same way that trailing branches bend under the weight of flowers in a hanging basket.

Conicals

Pillars and pyramids demand considerable skill of the grower. Conicals are easier to train, but produce spectacular results. This is another type of training associated with the Victorian period, and even experienced growers will often confuse it with the pyramid. The conical, however, offers a quicker and easier way to achieve a very similar shape.

Conicals should be at least 4 ft (120 cm) tall from soil to tip, and at least 2 ft (90 cm) wide at the base,. producing a more acute angle at the tip than the pyramid. A fully grown specimen will be some 6 ft (2 m) high and 3 ft (1 m) across at the base. If you have enough space in the greenhouse, the conical is a remarkably easy shape to grow. Start by selecting a vigorous, upright cultivar as early as possible from a cutting struck in early spring (see page 57), or from an autumn-struck cutting grown on in leaf during the winter. Your chosen cultivar should be one that produces plenty of self-branching side shoots; good choices include 'Fascination', 'Mrs Lovell Swisher', 'Display', 'Constance', 'Checkerboard', 'Blush of Dawn', 'Lena' and 'Cascade'.

Allow a single stem of the plant to grow erect, without the

slightest check (and without any stopping) until it reaches the intended height. As usual, pot on gradually, giving regular, nitrogen-rich feeds. Don't let the plant become potbound in the early stages of this rapid growth: premature flowering on the climbing shoot will slow its upward growth. The shoot will need some support. While it's in the 3 in (7.5 cm) and 4 in (10 cm) pots you should tie it loosely to a 30 in (75 cm) split cane. When it needs a larger pot, make sure the cane is taller than the main stem: you'll need one about 4–5 ft (120–150 cm) long.

The growth of side shoots is controlled with stops in the normal way. The lowest side shoots that develop on the middle of the main stem are stopped at two pairs of leaves. The uppermost side shoots are stopped at one pair of leaves. Shoots resulting from these stops can themselves be stopped at either one or two pairs of leaves, depending on the shape you want to achieve.

Growth should be rapid, so it's important to ensure regular feeding. Turn the plant frequently and regularly to ensure balanced growth on all sides. It will need plenty of space and head room; make sure it isn't overshadowed, or touching other plants. Good cultivation can easily produce a plant 5 ft (1.5 m) high in the first year; a conical this size should be in a 6 in (15 cm) or 7 in (18 cm) pot.

Right: *This 'Muriel' has been grown as a huge conical.*

Fuchsias as houseplants

Fuchsias aren't easy to grow as houseplants, mainly because few houses can provide them with the right growing conditions. Fuchsias like their roots cool and their heads in plenty of shade: they prefer a north- or northeast-facing window to one that faces south. And if fuchsias are to flower successfully indoors you must arrange to keep them moist but not wet, and in a humid environment.

If fuchsias drop all their buds and flowers when grown indoors, there is a simple reason for it: either the environment is wrong, or it has changed. A flowering fuchsia that has spent the best part of its life in a greenhouse, where the warmth and humidity are ideal, will never tolerate the dry atmosphere in most houses. Plants subjected to a sudden change in conditions will drop buds, flowers and even leaves. If this happens, take the plant out into the garden straight away, leave it in a shady place, and see that it doesn't lack for moisture. With plenty of spraying it will usually recover.

There are several ways to give indoor fuchsias the moisture they need. One is to put your potted fuchsia into a much larger pot (two or three sizes larger), and fill the surrounding space with sphagnum peat that is kept moist at all times. This method, called *double potting*, is used by some successful exhibitors to obtain their large specimen show plants. It's an excellent way of ensuring the right environment and humidity.

Another way to ensure humidity is to stand your fuchsia on a tray of damp gravel; sand is acceptable but dries out quickly. In either case, water the tray daily, but never stand the plant in a bowl or saucer of water. Any surplus must be drained away.

'Display' is perhaps the most suitable cultivar for growing as a houseplant.

Half-hardy and hardy fuchsias

It is not easy to grow fuchsias successfully indoors, but you can still admire them if they are just outside. Here on the patio is a three-tier 'Marinka'.

Fuchsias grow and flower better when they're grown outside than they do under glass. The fuchsia has been described as 'a tender greenhouse shrub', but this is hardly true. Most species are found on rain-drenched mountain slopes, or in dense evergreen forests, in regions which can be 7,000-15,000 ft (2,000-4,500 m) above sea level. At this altitude it's always cool, with plenty of moisture.

One of the species, *F. magellanica*, was found high up in the mountains in the southernmost part of South America, where the weather is often much worse than our own. The early hybridists used this species as a parent. As a result many of the modern hybrids and culti-

vars have some *magellanica* ancestry — one reason why fuchsias are much hardier than some people imagine. You don't need a greenhouse to grow good fuchsias.

Fuchsias can be grown outdoors:

- in pots or containers for patio, terrace or garden decoration (see page 50)

- as half-hardies in garden beds or borders (see page 51)

- as permanent shrubs or hedges (see page 53).

Fuchsias on a patio add to this colourful July display.

Indoor fuchsias, like their greenhouse counterparts, love to be sprayed with plain water. Again, this creates a moist atmosphere, but if the plants are in flower it tends to mark the blooms.

The best way of getting fuchsias to flower indoors is to raise your own cuttings, or to bring young, unflowered plants indoors very early in the season and grow them on in the exact position where you want them to flower. Don't give them too much water; remember that fuchsias like to be moist but not wet.

Half-hardies

Half-hardies produce the finest display. Make sure they've received the normal benefits of spring cultivation, pruning and so on. Check that the bed or the border is well prepared and well drained, and work in plenty of peat along with a 1-1-1 ratio fertiliser such as Growmore. You can start planting any time after the last frost; there are two possible methods:

- planting direct from pots (*in situ*)

- planting in the ground in pots.

Planting *in situ* produces the best display and cuts down the amount of watering you have to do. The plants produce a better root system, too, but in the autumn you'll have to lift them and pot them up in containers. On the other hand, the flowering period is longer and better, and autumn cuttings (if you want them) will be better and more prolific.

The second method (planting out the fuchsias in their pots) is easier, and because the roots are restricted the plants will flower earlier. The biggest advantage is seen in the autumn, when the plant in its pot can simply be lifted out of the ground. There, is, however, a disadvantage. Even when the pots are buried in soil up to the rim, they dry out surprisingly quickly. In moderate conditions use your hosepipe to keep the plants moist, and feed them regularly.

Whichever method you're using, plant deeply, preferably in semi-shade (somewhere that has sun in the morning and shade in the afternoon, or vice versa). Remember that fuchsias

'Apple Blossom' is an attractive half-hardy

have shallow roots; use your hoe and fork with great care, and do your weeding by hand.

Hardies

Hardies can be used as permanent shrubs in beds or borders, and on the rockery. They can even be used as screens or hedges. But do be careful: tall plants (e.g. standards and conicals) can't be thought of as permanent fixtures, and will not survive if they're left outside through the winter. This also goes for hardies that have been grown in containers and left on the patio. One frost will take out all the growth above soil level; container walls offer no protection at all.

You may be surprised to find how many hardy cultivars are now available: the various specialist nurseries in Britain offer more than 200. Gone are the days when red and purple were the only colours; now you can choose most colours including pinks, whites and even delicate pastel shades.

Prepare the ground as you would for the half-hardies,
ensuring there's good drainage, and digging in plenty of peat. Before planting, be sure you know just how high the plant will grow. The final height can range from 9 in (23 cm) to several metres, so a mistake could leave tall plants at the front of your border and dwarf plants at the back.

Hardies should be planted in the early summer, giving the plants time to become established before the autumn. Don't leave it till late summer or autumn, or the plant may not be sufficiently well established to survive the winter. If the plants are too small, they will not be suitable; they should adequately fill at least a 4 in (10 cm) pot. Plant several inches deeper than usual to protect the crown and roots from frost during the winter. This will also help produce early basal shoots the following spring. I recommend hollowing out a shallow hole some 3-4 in (7.5-10 cm) deep
and 9-10 in (23-25 cm) across. Make a deeper hole in the middle for the root ball and firm the plant in well, pressing strongly with your fingers. In due course watering and summer rain will bring the soil around the plant up to its normal height, but leaving the roots deeper, as they need to be.

The newly planted fuchsia must be kept moist all through the summer: this will help it to become established. Hardies should be allowed to finish their flowering naturally, so don't prune them heavily in the autumn (though trimming them down by about a third will do no harm). The remaining growth will give a certain amount of protection against frost. Even in a severe winter it shouldn't be necessary to cover the crown of a hardy, but should you wish to do so, use peat, sand or old potting compost. Leaves are not really suitable, as they tend to blow away. You can remove this protection in the spring, when the new growth appears and the old growth is cut back to soil level.

One final word of warning. Once they're established, hardies dislike being moved or having their roots disturbed. Remember that their roots are shallow, so tidying and weeding should not be done with anything larger than a hand fork.

'Beacon Rosea'

In pots and containers

The best plants for this purpose are two-, three- or four-year-olds that have been grown in frost-free conditions and then pruned, repotted and potted on.

The best time to put them outside will depend on where you are and what the weather is like. Under normal conditions the right time would be towards

Above: *An old tree stump makes a fascinating and unusual container.*

Left: *'Waveney Sunrise' in an urn flanked by smaller plants*

the middle or end of April. Put them where they can receive as much sun as possible but are protected from cold winds. The plants are in pots, so if there's any chance of frost it's easy enough to shelter them or to protect them overnight with some suitable covering. When the frosts have passed you can put the plants in their summer positions. A semi-shaded spot is ideal, but they'll tolerate full sun if they have to. Once the plants are well established the pots will dry out quickly, so do make sure they're kept moist. They'll need frequent watering.

Beds and borders

Growing conditions in Britain are surprisingly similar to those in the fuchsia's natural habitat: the roots remain cool, and there is some shade for top growth. So where better to grow your fuchsias than in the beds and borders of your own garden? The fuchsia's versatility makes it suitable for many different planting schemes, but it's most popular as a half-hardy, bedded out with other flowering and foliage plants.

Certain colours perform better than others in these conditions. Red and purple flowers will thrive anywhere, and so will the 'red and whites'. Orange-coloured fuchsias are generally sun-loving, and these include the triphyllas (nearly all the triphyllas have orange or orange-red flowers). White flowers, like the 'pink and whites', are very demanding. All prefer shade: whites will become pink, bordering on rosy red, if they're permanently exposed to the sunlight.

Trailing fuchsias are totally unsuitable for planting in beds. Variegated and ornamental foliage fuchsias are a much better choice, since they flourish where there is plenty of light but like as little moisture as possible. 'Cloth of Gold' and 'Tom West' make good bushes but are frost-shy; *F. magellanica* var. *gracilis variegata* and 'Genii' are attractive and hardy.

Planting fuchsias as bedding plants is very convenient, since they can go in at the same time as other early summer bedders. The plants will have spent the previous few months in the congenial conditions of the greenhouse, so they need to be reasonably hardened off before planting. Ideally they should be coming into bud, but not yet flowering, and growing in 5 in (13 cm) pots. If they're in anything smaller, you'll have to wait while they make growth and roots before they come into flower.

For the best results plant them *in situ* (see page 48); if you plant them out in their pots instead, bury them up to the rim. The height of the plants is obviously very important, especially if they are central in beds, or at the rear of borders. Make sure they have shade at some point in the day. Fuchsias don't respond well to the hot midday sun, or to hot, drying winds.

Fuchsias make a wonderful contribution to any garden.

Bedding schemes

An ideal scheme could incorporate half and full standards (securely staked) dotted liberally among ground cover of the best bedding annuals. A brilliant display can be obtained using 'Bon Accorde'; 'Celia Smedley'; 'Barbara' and 'Snowcap' as standards, with *Begonia semperflorens* 'Organdy' interspersed with the cineraria *Senecio maritima* 'Silver Dust'. Other equally good bedding plants are impatiens of the F1 Accent series, which can be used to great effect with heliotrope marine. The F1 ageratum interplanted with alyssum is very effective. 'Crystal Palace' lobelia blends well with 'Organdy'

begonias, while French and American F1 marigolds are extremely weather-tolerant. The F1 Express series petunias do exceptionally well in tubs, as well as providing a blanket of bedding colour. Fiery red salvias add that touch of vivid display and contrast well with most fuchsias. If you are thinking of

Fuchsias in half-baskets form a lovely backdrop to this glorious garden scheme.

mass planting with dwarf fuchsias for a bed, or for ground cover, consider the 'Thumb' family: 'Tom'; 'Lady' and 'Son of' grow no higher than 12 in (30 cm). The 'Seven Dwarves' ('Happy', 'Doc', 'Sleepy', 'Sneezy', 'Bashful', 'Grumpy' and 'Dopey') are only 9-15 in (23-38 cm) tall, and like the 'Thumbs' all are hardy.

An attractive bedding scheme: standard fuchsias, including three of 'Bon Accorde' (left) and one of 'Phyllis' (centre, red), with salvias (red) and 'Crystal Palace' lobelias in front.

Growing fuchsias as hedges

The fuchsia as a hardy plant, especially for hedges, has never been used as much as it could be. As long as you don't plant it in a frost pocket, it should survive in almost every part of the British Isles.

Many people may have seen hedgerow fuchsias in Devon and Cornwall, on the west coast of Scotland, and in County Kerry on the west coast of Ireland. In these places the species *F. magellanica*, with its variants *alba* (*molinea*), *globosa*, *gracilis*, *riccartonii* (sometimes regarded as a cultivar, 'Riccartonii') and *thompsonii*, has become naturalised, flowering from mid-summer to autumn. The fuchsia can be used as a low hedge, for edging or dividing purposes, or even (with the right choice of cultivars) to create a sizeable screen or hedge several feet high.

The ideal spot for a fuchsia hedge will depend on the local climate. Ideally this should be cool, moist and humid, with shade at some part of the day. The site should be sheltered from hot, dry winds, which will cause scorching and dry out the leaves.

Fuchsia hardies for hedges will grow in most soils, but you'll need to prepare the site before you plant them. The best time to do this is late autumn or early winter, so the soil can weather before the planting. Although fuchsias have shallow roots, they need a deep, cool root run, so dig deep (about 20-24 in/50-60 cm down) to break up the subsoil. If this subsoil is loose, add peat or humus of some description. If, on the other hand, it is clayey and heavy, add gravel or sand to prevent waterlogging. If you can get farmyard manure, work it into the bottom 10-12 in (25-30 cm) of the hole. When filling up the hole you can use moisture-retaining material such as peat, spent hops, humus or manure to good advantage.

Plant the fuchsias in late spring, when there's no further danger of frost. This gives them the whole summer to establish themselves and to prepare for the winter. On no account plant any hardy fuchsia in late summer or early autumn. They won't have time to become established, and are certain to be lost during the winter.

Order your plants from the nurseryman well in advance, and take delivery in pots no smaller than 3½ in (9 cm). Do remember that hardies are available in colours other than red and purple. If you can grow them on to 4¼ in (11 cm) or 5 in (13 cm) pots your chances of success will improve, but only if the plants have been hardened off before planting. Don't forget, or the foliage will start to turn bronze and the leaves will begin to fall. To harden off the plants, transfer them to a garden frame, still in their pots, two or three

'La Campanella'

53

weeks before planting. Keep the frame closed to start with, but you should open it a little at a time until you can remove the top light completely.

Planting distances will vary according to the vigour of the cultivars, but 18 in (45 cm) between plants is usually about right. It's important to plant the fuchsias with the top of the roots at least 2 in (5 cm) below soil level to protect the roots from frost damage. Fuchsias need to be firmly planted, with no air pockets, so tread the soil in lightly around each plant with the heel of your boot. They won't need fertiliser or feed at this stage, though it may be worth digging in a little bone-meal around the roots. Water

the plants in well. If the weather is dry after planting, water them regularly to stop the soil drying out. The plants should be sprayed from above, or watered from above using a fine-rosed watering can.

During the first winter, cover the base of your plants with peat, sand or leaves. This will protect the roots from frost, and can be removed in the spring. Don't prune the plants in the autumn or during the first winter. By leaving intact all the growth they have made during the summer, you will provide a little protection against bad weather.

Prune the plants in early or late spring, when new growth appears at the base. If this new

growth has been taken by the frosts, prune right down to ground level; otherwise prune back to those shoots appearing low down on the stems or laterals.

During the second summer the hedge should achieve the growth and colour you want. You can feed the plants considerably more during this second year. Start with a high-nitrogen feed and then change to a high-potassium feed when the buds and flowers appear.

Once established, fuchsia hardies don't like to be moved or to have their roots disturbed: remember that their roots are shallow. Any weeding should be done by hand rather than with a hoe.

Cultivars suitable as hedges

Cultivar	Bloom	Colour	Height
'Brilliant'	single	Red and purple	2½ ft (75 cm)
'Caledonia'	single	Red and purple	2 ft (60 cm)
'Chillerton Beauty'	single	Rose-pink/mauve violet	2 ft (60 cm)
'Dr Foster'	single	Scarlet and violet	3½ ft (1 m)
'Flash'	single	Light magenta and red	2½ ft (75 cm)
F. magellanica var. *alba*	single	White and very pale lilac	6-10 ft (1.8-3 m)
var. *gracilis*	single	Deep red and purple	4-8 ft (1.2-2.4 m)
var. *riccartonii*	single	Scarlet and dark purple	4-6 ft (1.2-1.8 m)
var. *thompsonii*	single	Red and purple	4-5 ft (1.2-1.5 m)
'Graf Witte'	single	Carmine and purple rose	3 ft (90 cm)
'Margaret'	single	Carmine and violet	3-4 ft (90-120 cm)
'Mrs Popple'	single	Scarlet and purple violet	2-3 ft (60-90 cm)
'Phyllis'	single	Waxy rose and cerise	3 ft (90 cm)
'Prosperity'	double	Crimson and pale rose	3 ft (90 cm)
'Whiteknight's Pearl'	single	White and pale pink	4 ft (1.2 m)

Right: 'Orchid Flame'

Seeds and cuttings

Fuchsias aren't just easy to cultivate, they're also one of the easiest plants to propagate. Seeds or cuttings are normally used; grafting is rare, unless a slow-growing cultivar or a weak grower is needed as a standard.

Seed

Sowing seeds is the only way to produce new cultivars; apart from the species, no fuchsia will come true to type. Since there are now some 10,000 different cultivars, the chance of producing something entirely new is fairly remote (unless, that is, you undertake some very selective hybridising). If, however, you'd like to try, sow as soon as possible after ripening. Don't expect many flowers until the second year. You'll need to grow the plants for another year or two after that, to check that any new characteristics won't revert to those of the parent plants.

Taking cuttings

Most propagated fuchsias are grown from cuttings. This is the only way to create an exact replica of the original plant. There are two types of cuttings. The *normal cutting* has three or four pairs of leaves and will be about 3-4 in (7.5-10 cm) long. A *tip cutting* consists of the tip and one pair of leaves.

Under the right conditions cuttings can be struck (see page 57) at any time, but why not choose your time for taking them carefully in order to get the best results? Softwood cuttings taken in the early months of the year are easily the best. Hardwood cuttings taken in the autumn are not so reliable, and take much longer to root.

Some cuttings in a seed tray with some of the tools you'll need.

Above: *A tip cutting consists of the shoot tip and just one leaf pair.*

Left: *A normal cutting includes three or four leaf pairs.*

Successful rooting depends on what you do in the first stages. Never take cuttings unless they are strong and healthy on the mother plant. Always take and strike cuttings in complete shade, never in hot sun, and always make your cut just above a node or joint, as this is where the greatest concentration of hormones is. Use a very sharp blade and make clean, accurate cuts, with no jagged edges.

Never take cuttings with buds or flowers present. The cutting needs all its energy for rooting, so it has none to spare for flowering. If buds or flowers *are* present, remove them, but do remember that these cuttings may take longer to root.

Striking cuttings

If you've taken a normal cutting, use your blade to trim off all but the top pair of leaves and the tip. Cut just below the joint in each case, leaving a clean stem. This should not be too long, or it tends to rot. Before you put the cutting into a striking medium, bathe it in a mixture of water and Benlate. This eliminates any risk of damping-off or botrytis. Even if you don't use Benlate, bathe the cuttings in clear water for about a minute while you're writing the label. You can use rooting powder if you wish, but it isn't really necessary.

Now put the cuttings in a *shallow* container (e.g. a seed tray or half pot) filled with equal parts of washed sand (or

Coffee jars make the cheapest propagators.

grit) and sphagnum peat. The sand *must* be washed, and the peat *must* be sphagnum. An even better mixture is four parts Humber soilless compost to one part perlite. When striking, use a dibber or similar instrument: never *push* cuttings into the medium. With normal cuttings, about half the length of the cutting should be in the medium. With tip cuttings, as much as possible should be covered. In some cases you'll only be able to see the tip sitting on the surface of the medium. Firm in well in either case, so as not to leave any air pockets.

Water the cuttings well in with a *rosed* can and put them in a propagator of some kind. If possible, arrange for a soil-warming cable to provide heat from the bottom. Shade the cuttings from direct sunlight, and use a suitable lid to help create a moist, humid atmosphere.

Encouraging cuttings to root

From now on the cuttings must *never* be allowed to wilt or dry out. Spray them regularly with clear water according to the prevailing conditions; you might have to do this once or even twice a day to maintain the right environment.

With bottom heat, the cuttings should start to produce roots after about 12–14 days. Without bottom heat this will take about 28 days. Rooting times vary according to the prevailing conditions; in April or May, when conditions are very favourable, they could be considerably shorter.

Continue to shade the cuttings from direct sunlight throughout the rooting period. After about three weeks, unheated cuttings

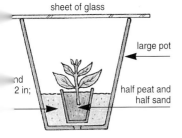

sheet of glass

large pot

nd 2 in;

half peat and half sand

An inexpensive propagator

should take on a darker, perky look. Now you can allow some air into the propagator, closing it down at nightfall. Gradually increase the air supply until the cuttings can be removed for potting on (into the smallest possible pot).

Cuttings can easily be rooted in water, but this will produce extremely brittle roots, so I don't recommend this method unless it's absolutely necessary. Don't use fertiliser at any time during the rooting period. You can give the plants a weak feed after they have been established in their pots for about three weeks.

If you follow these methods, you should expect nothing less than a 99 per cent success rate.

Above: *These well-rooted cuttings should each be potted in a container of the size shown.*

Below: *This superior early growth has come from tip cuttings.*

Sports and mutations

Sports and mutations are not a method of propagation — there is no way to *make* them happen — but they have produced many attractive features.

Sports and mutations are a sudden variation, caused by changes in the plant's chromosomes or genes that produce offspring different from its parents. Some fuchsias, for instance, have changed their leaf colouring through mutation, while the flowers remain the same as the original plant. *F. magellanica* var. *gracilis variegata*, for instance, has silvery, variegated foliage. 'Golden Marinka' has bright-coloured foliage, banded and splashed with cream and gold. Both plants are quite distinct from their parents.

Most sports are best exemplified by colour changes in the corolla. The change is generally from a dark colour to a lighter colour: good examples of this are 'Lady Thumb' (from 'Tom Thumb') and 'Cardinal Farges' (from 'Abbé Farges'). Very occasionally there is a reverse change from a light to a darker colour.

Sports and mutations are extremely interesting phenomena, producing many worthwhile new additions to the vast list of cultivars.For example, the first white corollas, the first marbling effects, and the first white-tubed fuchsia, 'Venus Victrix', were all the result of natural mutations.

A sport — note the change in colour of the corollas.

59

Soils and composts

It's important to cultivate fuchsias in the right medium. They will grow in almost any soil, but ordinary garden soil will give only poor results.

Soil is the upper part of the earth's land surface, 4–18 in (10–45 cm) deep, on which plant life grows. It is made up of crushed rock, decayed vegetation and animal remains, and contains *humus*, the 'body' of all soils and compost. Soils may be clayey, sandy or chalky. The ideal soil, sought out by gardeners for the cultivation of their plants, is called *loam*: it contains more or less equal parts of sand, silt and clay, and is usually rich in humus.

Plants in pots are best grown in *compost*. The word 'compost' is confusing because it has two different meanings:

• a balanced mixture of different kinds of soil for the cultivation of plants grown in pots or containers

• a valuable material made by rotting down vegetable or plant refuse.

Throughout this book we have used the word 'compost' in its first meaning.

The ideal compost (especially for fuchsias) should:

• retain moisture, but be well drained

• contain humus, and the food or fertilisers that the plant requires.

The best potting compost for fuchsias is a John Innes, but do be sure it's good-quality compost mixed to the original John Innes formula. The right mix is 7 parts loam to 3 parts peat and 2 parts sand (with the parts measured by bulk, not weight). A measured quantity of John Innes Base Fertiliser is added to this mix. For John Innes No. 1, add 4 oz (110 g) to every 8 gallon (36 l) batch of your mix. For No. 2, add 8 oz (225 g), and

for No. 3, 12 oz (350 g). No. 2 is probably the best for fuchsias.

These composts rely on a high-quality loam. Loam for compost must be sterilised either by steam or with chemicals. This is not a job for the inexperienced: partial sterilisation is much more dangerous than no sterilisation at all.

The pH (a figure indicating acidity or alkalinity) is important, too. A pH of 7.0 indicates a neutral state: loam for compost should have a pH of 6.8, i.e. very slightly acidic.

Be sure to use John Innes composts within eight weeks of mixing. If they're left any longer, the chemical reactions in the compost cause a build-up of ammonia, which turns the mixture alkaline.

'Sapphire'

- they are chemically uniform and relatively inert

- they retain water well

- they do not readily become compacted

- they are lighter in weight

- they are clean and simple to handle.

There are, however, some disadvantages:

- Watering can be a problem, especially if you're using plastic pots. It's easy to over-water, but if compost is allowed to become really dry it can be difficult to get it moist again. You may have to water two, three or even four times to get the results you need.

- Some soilless composts are too loose and light to suit fuchsia growers. Plants with average top growth can become top heavy, while any compost that doesn't include a certain amount of grit or similar material can make staking a problem.

It's up to you which compost you use, but for cultivating specimen plants I would strongly recommend John Innes compost in clay pots.

One final word of warning. Since both types of compost are made to specific formulas, *never* attempt to mix the two.

I'm sure that you can now see why it is so important to have a good source of John Innes compost.

Even so, if you can obtain a good loam, and you don't mind a few weeds, fuchsias won't object to unsterilised loam. Make up your own mixtures with a formula of two parts loam, one part sphagnum peat and one part coarse sand or crushed gravel. Add 4 oz (110 g) of John Innes Base Fertiliser to every 8 gallons (36 l) of your mix.

Left: *A well-equipped potting bench with a ready supply of potting compost*

Another possible alternative is one of the *soilless* composts. There are several proprietary brands, including Arthur Bowers, Humber and Levington. All are suitable for fuchsia cultivation. Most use the D1 mix recommended by the University of California. This consists of 75 per cent pure sphagnum peat and 25 per cent pure washed silicate quartz sand. Chemical fertilisers and balanced amounts of trace elements are added to this mix.

Soilless composts offer several advantages:

- they have an indefinite storage life, and do not deteriorate

Feeding and fertilisers

Fuchsias are heavy feeders and must be properly fed, especially when they're established and in flower. Without feeding they'll produce fewer flowers, and those they do produce will be small.

Plants can make their own starch and protein as long as certain chemicals are available to the root system. The minute hairs just behind the tip of the root form the 'mouth' of the plant. You can start a young plant on a weak feed as soon as it's established in its first pot. You can standardise feeding by using the same calculated strength of fertiliser throughout the season; simply feed the plant more often instead of increasing the strength of the fertiliser. This makes it possible to feed the plant every time you water it, but the feed solution should be very weak.

Never feed plants when they're dry at the roots (because this burns up the small, hairy roots), and never feed sickly-looking plants. Fuchsias can be overfed. This will cause lush growth, especially if the plant is also over-potted. Never apply any fertiliser other than according to the instructions on the label.

Feed your fuchsia seedlings correctly, and they can produce flowers with beautifully curled sepals like these.

Fertilisers are classified as *organic* and *inorganic*. Organic fertilisers are obtained from animal or vegetable sources. Inorganic fertilisers are artificial and manufactured. Both are important plant foods containing three key nutrients, nitrogen, phosphorus and potassium (abbreviated to their chemical symbols N, P and K). All proprietary fertilisers contain these nutrients, and the numbers on the label are used to indicate the percentage of each in the mix. 9-6-4, for instance, indicates a mix with 9 per cent nitrogen (N), 6 per cent phosphorus (P) and 4 per cent potassium (K). The content varies from brand to brand, but the NPK ratio is always quoted as prescribed by law.

It's useful to understand what these nutrients are and do.

Nitrogen (N)
Nitrogen is the most essential nutrient, stimulating leaf growth as well as growth in the stem and laterals, which increases the size of the plant. Stunted plants with small, pale leaves may well be suffering from nitrogen deficiency.

Organic sources of nitrogen include bonemeal, hoof and horn meal and dried blood. Inorganic sources include ammonium sulphate and sodium nitrate, both of which provide a rapid release of nitrogen.

Phosphorus (P)
Phosphorus stimulates the growth of the root system and speeds up flowering. Plants with a deficiency will grow slowly, appearing stunted, with poorly developed, dull or yellowed leaves. Superphosphate of lime is a quick-acting inorganic fertiliser; bonemeal is slow-acting and organic.

Potassium (K)

Don't be confused by the chemical symbol K, which is derived from the modern Latin word *kalium*. Potassium is essential for plants: without it they can't make full use of nitrogen. It helps to prevent soft growth, improves the colour of flowers and increases resistance to disease. Signs of potassium deficiency include scorching at the edges of leaves and a reduced number of small, poorly coloured flowers. Potassium sulphate is a quick-acting inorganic fertiliser with a high potassium content. Wood ash is an organic alternative, but the potassium concentration is low.

Now you know the function of each nutrient, it's possible to look at a balanced feeding programme. In the early stages of growth, to early or mid-summer, use a high-nitrogen fertiliser with a ratio of 3-1-1, 3-0-1, 3-2-1 or similar. When buds and flowers start to appear, change to a high-potassium fertiliser with a ratio of 1-1-3, 1-0-3, 1-2-3 or similar. During the short period (about three weeks) just before the plant is budding, and just after it has started, use a balanced fertiliser with the ratio 1-1-1.

'Cecile'

Recommended fertilisers with ratios

Brand name	Nitrogen %	Phosphorus %	Potassium %	Ratio (approx.)
Bio Instant	15	15	25	1-1-2
Bio Plant Food	5.2	5.2	6	1-1-1
Boots General	9.3	6.8	4.2	3-2-1
Boots Tomato	4	4	7	1-1-2
Chempak no. 2	25	15	15	2-1-1
Chempak no. 3	20	20	20	1-1-1
Chempak no. 4	15	15	30	1-1-2
Chempak no. 8	12.5	25	25	1-2-2
Growmore	7	7	7	1-1-1
John Innes Base	5.1	7.2	9.7	1-2-3
Liquinure	9	6.6	4.1	3-2-1
Phostrogen	9.7	10	26.5	1-1-3
Vitax Vitafeed 101	26	0	26	1-0-1
Vitax Vitafeed 102	18	0	36	1-0-2
Vitax Vitafeed 103	13	0	43	1-0-3
Vitax Vitafeed 301	36	0	12	3-0-1

Trace elements

Trace elements are found in all good composts. One very important one is magnesium (Mg). The supply of magnesium becomes exhausted when plants are grown in the same compost for more than a year, especially if they aren't repotted. If leaves have yellow streaks and spots, and are starting to fall, magnesium deficiency may be the problem. If it's left untreated the leaves will turn completely yellow and decay will set in. The remedy is 1 tablespoon (30 ml) of magnesium sulphate (Epsom Salts) to 1 gallon (4.5 l) of water, applied two or three times at intervals of a week. Yellowing upper leaves may be a sign of deficiency in another trace element, iron. The remedy is two or three applications of ferrous sulphate at weekly intervals, again in the ratio 1 tablespoon (30 ml) of ferrous sulphate to 1 gallon (4.5 l) of water.

Organic fertilisers

There are few nutrients in animal manure, so the NPK values are very low. A ton (1 tonne) of decayed stable manure contains just 11 lb (5 kg) of nitrogen (0.5 per cent), 8 lb (3.5 kg) of phosphorus (0.35 per cent), 12 lb (5.5 kg) of potassium (0.55 per cent) and 16 lb (7.25 kg) of calcium (0.725 per cent). All the rest is either moisture or humus, and it's the humus that gives the greatest benefit to the soil when the manure is dug in.

Slow-release fertilisers are comparatively new. The rate of

The yellow leaves are a serious sign of magnesium deficiency.

release depends on the temperature: release only takes place in significant amounts if the air temperature is around 70°F (21°C) or higher. The advantage is that one application will last right through the growing season. Two popular feeds are both marketed under the brand name Osmocote. One, with an NPK of 18-11-10, is a coated granular fertiliser released over 6–9 months. The other (better for fuchsias) has an NPK of 14-14-14, and offers controlled, short-term release over 3–4 months.

Right: *'Orange Drops'*

64

Watering

It has been said that if you can master the watering can you're three-quarters of the way towards successful cultivation. I have to admit that after many years I'm still trying. Why do we water, and what happens when we do?

Watering moistens the soil, and so releases the mineral salts that plants take up as food. These salts, dissolved in the water, are absorbed through the root hairs and drawn up into the body of the plant. The nutrients are retained to nourish the plant. The plant tissues need the water too, of course. Water is

This unfortunate plant has suffered sun scorch compounded by later moisture damage.

gradually transpired through the leaves. The process is continuous, and the water must be replaced all the time.

When you are watering cuttings, rooted cuttings, repotted or potted-on plants, it's always best to water from above, using a fine-rosed can. This method settles the soil, and prevents the topsoil hardening or caking. Watering plants like these direct from the spout is never a good idea: it will disturb the soil, create air pockets and unsettle newly planted plants. However, if the plant is established and well rooted in its final pot, watering direct from the spout should do no harm.

It's very difficult to say how often a plant should be watered. The answer depends on many

factors: the size of the greenhouse, the amount of root action, the weather conditions, the size of the plant, the size of the pot (and whether it's made of clay or plastic), and the situation. It's also important to remember that a newly potted plant needs far less water than one that is well established; in general you can say that the smaller the pot, the less watering it needs.

With considerable experience you can tell if a plant needs water simply by looking at it. Tapping the pot with a stick (or your knuckles) was never infallible, even when all pots were made of clay, and it doesn't work at all with plastic pots. The best, and most accurate, method is to test the weight of each pot individually. If it feels heavy, it doesn't need water; if it feels light, it does need water; if it's 'in between', leave it till next time.

The ideal time to water is just before the plant needs it, but in practice this is none too easy to determine. Even so, it's important to try. Plants only grow well when they have the right amount of water: overwatered or underwatered plants are not going to grow as they should.

Treat all your plants as individuals, and water them as necessary. It's thoroughly bad gardening practice to treat a whole batch of plants in exactly the same way. Always water from the top, and very rarely from the bottom. Saucers are a luxury to all plants: if there's any water

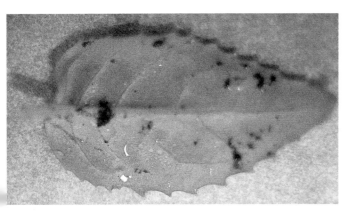

Overwatering can be just as lethal as underwatering, and this leaf shows clear signs of moisture damage.

the soil ball on an upturned pot until the compost is no longer too moist. Symptoms of overwatering are yellow leaves, wilting and leaf drop. (Do remember, though, that wilting can be caused by other problems, including underwatering and too high a temperature.)

Tap water is invariably cold, and in most areas it is hard, because of its lime content. Fuchsias don't particularly care for lime, though they will tolerate it. On the whole it's better if you can arrange to collect soft rainwater.

left in the saucer after watering, drain it off. Always try to finish watering before early afternoon at the latest. The ideal time is during the morning.

Never water at night unless it's absolutely necessary. It may be the only time you can manage it, but it's still very bad practice. You're simply adding to the moisture already present in the night air: moisture that cannot be absorbed, and which can cause flowers and blooms to damp off and buds to fall.

Most beginners in the greenhouse are guilty of overwatering, which (perhaps surprisingly) kills more plants than underwatering. Watch your watering technique if you are using soilless composts in plastic pots. It's all too easy to overwater, so be sure to lift the pots and test their weight first.

If you've overwatered a plant, take it out of its pot and stand

Below: *'Moyra'*

Environment

Temperature

Many aspects of fuchsia cultivation are carried out in the shelter of the greenhouse, where temperature is of prime importance.

Most fuchsias will die if they're exposed to frost. Hardy cultivars *can* survive, but only if their roots are protected by fairly deep planting. Any fuchsia, hardy or not, that's planted in a container and left outside will be vulnerable to frost penetrating the container walls. Even hardies grown in pots under glass will succumb. If plants have suffered frost damage their foliage will become limp and eventually turn black. The damage is caused by ice crystals forming inside the cells of the plant. When the ice melts, the volume of liquid inside the cell expands, distorting or rupturing the cell wall. This leaves the plant drooping and glassy-looking.

Too much heat, on the other hand, will break down and deactivate the proteins in the plant — and any plant will lose considerable amounts of moisture in hot conditions. If the water isn't replaced because the soil is dry, or because the leaves are losing moisture faster than the roots can replace it, the whole plant will wilt. The cells lose so much moisture that they shrink, and the leaves become limp.

A minimum and maximum thermometer is essential for greenhouse cultivation, but be careful where you put it. Hanging it in a sunny position will produce odd readings, and it won't be accurate if it's too close to the glass. The ideal position is one where the air is representative of the air in the whole greenhouse, preferably in the shade, and at the same height as the plants.

A temperature of 33–34°F (1°C) is enough to keep fuchsias comfortable while they're stored over the winter. For the rest of the year they prefer an equable temperature, with a little (but not too much) variation between day and night. An ideal temperature for the summer months is a pleasant and tolerable 60–70°F (16–21°C). Fuchsias can cope with higher tempera-tures, but they stop growing if the thermometer climbs above 77°F (25°C), so you must be able to reduce the temperature with shading and ventilation. Excellent displays can be grown under glass, but in the heat of summer it's better to move your plants outside. Find them a shady spot where they'll be protected from the wind.

Shading

If you are growing fuchsias under glass, shading is essential to control the temperature of the greenhouse during hot weather to keep it below 77°F (25°C).

Slatted blinds are ideal but very expensive. Green poly-

Plastic netting gives protection against wasps, bees and hot sunshine, but at the same time allows air and moisture to pass through.

This unusual shade house has been built out of fluorescent tubing.

thene blinds fitted inside the glass are quite effective, but will play havoc with your perception of colour. There are several types of plastic mesh that give excellent results, but never lay the mesh flat on the glass; leave at least 1 in (2.5 cm) between the glass and the mesh, or you'll increase the heat instead of reducing it.

Most enthusiasts resort to permanent shading. White is the best colour, as it reflects back more heat. The cheapest method is to mix ordinary plain flour or whitening with water, adding a little salt to help the adhesion. Decorators' size is even better.

Apply your shading early. It's a good idea to start with a thin layer around Easter, then add an extra coat when the plants are more mature (i.e. when they are budding and flowering).

I can also recommend Varishade, developed by Solar Sunstill Inc. in America and available from most gardening shops and centres. When dry, it provides very effective shade, filtering out excessive light and heat. If it gets wet (from rain, for example), it will become almost transparent until the coating dries again.

If Varishade is applied to the inner surface of the glass it will be kept transparent in the early morning (often until around 10 am) by the normal condensation inside the greenhouse. This is particularly useful in spring, in early summer and in autumn.

Varishade is non-toxic, and can be sprayed or brushed on (though I prefer to use a roller).

It can easily be removed by washing down the glass.

My second choice would be Coolglass. This mixes instantly with cold water, can be sprayed or brushed on easily, and produces a white coating. It won't get washed away by the rain, it's harmless to plants, and it won't contaminate any rain water you are collecting, yet it can be removed with the flick of a duster.

Shade houses can be made out of polythene or plastic green netting, but polythene creates condensation problems. Woven plastic netting is excellent. It doesn't cause condensation, and allows air to pass through. It also admits natural rainfall and morning dews, and the mesh is usually too small for wasps and bees to gain entry. It provides as much light as possible on dull days, yet also gives effective shading in high summer.

Ventilation

If you're growing fuchsias under glass, ventilation is as important as any other aspect of cultivation. Many growers treat their fuchsias as tender greenhouse shrubs, forgetting that *F. magellanica*, from which many of our modern cultivars were bred, was found at the southern extremity of Chile around the Straits of Magellan. The fuchsia is far hardier than many people think, and benefits from as much air as possible in the greenhouse. You should, however, try to avoid draughts. If you forget to open the ventilators on a hot sunny morning, never rush into the greenhouse in a panic and throw open all the ventilators and doors. Take your time, and provide ventilation in easy stages.

Pre-war greenhouses were better constructed than many modern houses, and usually included roof, stage and floor ventilators. To cut costs, the modern, small greenhouse is usually sold with a single top ventilator. When this is opened the colder, heavier air entering the greenhouse sinks down, pushing the lighter, warm air out through the ventilator. Except on a very warm day, this creates a cold draught that is likely to damage your plants.

Ideally you should have ventilators in the roof, at stage level and at ground level, as well as a door at each end of the greenhouse. In hot weather open the roof vents first: these will remove the stale air and allow a slow circulation. Now open the stage vents. This will create a rising current of air from the eaves to the ridge, cooling the greenhouse and drying up any condensation on the glass. Floor vents should be used only occasionally, to allow a current of air to circulate freely around the plants themselves. Opening the doors allows air to pass right through the building. Don't do this except on very hot days with very little wind, or you risk losing all the humidity in the greenhouse. A sliding door is much better than the conventional door for keeping internal temperatures and humidity right. It can be used as a large ventilator, and it's easy to adjust as required.

Automatic vents regulate the flow of air to achieve a pre-set temperature.

The top vents should remain open all summer, while the side louvres can be adjusted to the breeze outside.

Ventilate early in the day, so that the temperature inside your greenhouse can return to normal before the outside air becomes cooler. Your timetable will obviously vary from one season to the next, but always use ventilators with discretion; remember that fuchsias thrive in

fresh air, but also need a humid atmosphere.

Fuchsias should be grown as hard as possible. That means your top vents should be open by late spring (unless there's a risk of high winds), and should stay open till mid-autumn. Use stage vents judiciously; don't open them fully except on very warm days. You might think about fitting louvres in the sides of your greenhouse; if the breeze outside is strong, you can adjust the opening so there are no direct draughts.

If you need to arrange ventilation while you're away from home, think about buying automatic vent openers. These devices open your ventilators in response to a sudden rise in temperature: they'll usually start to operate at 60°F (16°C), but they can be adjusted. They don't need electricity, and they don't need complex fittings. Automatic vent openers are normally fitted to the roof ventilators, but can be used for side vents. Each unit can lift about 15 lb (7 kg).

An exchange of air inside the greenhouse encourages better growth and prevents stagnant air (which can make the plants vulnerable to disease). Electric fans (either the fan part of a greenhouse heater or a dedicated fan) will move the air efficiently. Extractor fans will ensure a good exchange of air: aim for 20–30 changes per hour.

Pruning

The point of pruning fuchsias is to control the size of the plant, and to ensure there's plenty of new wood. Fuchsias bloom only on new wood, so growth from the base should be encouraged, especially in bushes and trailers. Pruning assists this growth, but do remember that the fuchsia is a shrub, and needs about three months' complete rest over the winter. At the end of this period prune the old wood back to force the new growth.

Left to themselves, fuchsias will normally finish flowering between September and early November. During this period it's quite important to stand them outside (or to give them full ventilation if they're staying in the greenhouse). This has the important effect of ripening soft, green growth; and plants that have been ripened off have a much better chance of surviving the winter.

If you wish, you can prune fuchsias very lightly in early autumn to improve their shape before they're brought indoors. It's best to avoid anything more:

the sap will be high in the stem, or flowing, and is bound to seep out after hard (or even moderate) pruning. This may cause excessive dieback as it spreads downward. Unripened wood is particularly vulnerable. Another risk with autumn pruning becomes apparent in a mild, early winter. In these conditions the plants are likely to make new growth at a time when they should be resting. Some growers have found a successful method of autumn pruning that obviously produces good results for them, but it must be done when the sap is falling, and the cuts must dry out quickly.

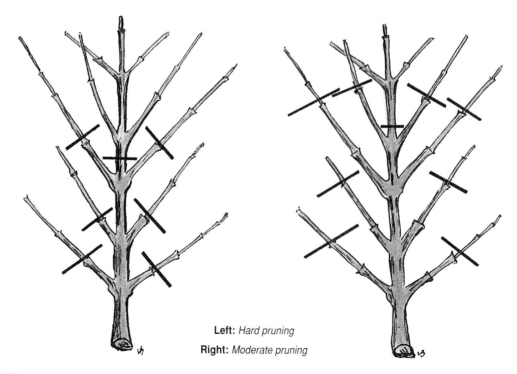

Left: *Hard pruning*
Right: *Moderate pruning*

It's difficult to recommend the best time for pruning; in general, most experienced growers prefer to do it just before the sap starts to rise (i.e. during January, February and March). The exact timing will depend on the heating available in your greenhouse. If you're willing to use large amounts of heat, plants can be started into growth in January, with moderate heat in February, and little heat (other than that provided by the sun) through March.

Begin by spraying your plants with clear, tepid water as soon as conditions allow it. Before long the new buds will have developed enough to indicate where the new shoots are going to grow. This is the right time to prune, because now it's possible to shape the plants. In general, cut back about two-thirds of the previous year's growth, removing all dead wood and spindly growth; in most cases this will leave two or three joints or nodes on each lateral. Prune standards back harder than bush plants, to encourage tighter growth. Trailers and basket-grown plants also need hard pruning to produce new growth from the base. Don't prune back outdoor hardies in the autumn or during the winter. Wait till new growth appears at the base in early spring, then prune back hard, almost to soil level.

Stopping and pinching fuchsias

For the new enthusiast, stopping and pinching out is probably the most challenging aspect of cultivation. Where and when do you do it?

Every stop will help to increase the size of the plant, but will also delay flowering by several weeks. With care, you can arrange for plants to flower at a specified time; but to produce a well-shaped plant with the best possible growth and the largest possible number of flowers, you'll need to pinch out several times.

A lateral shoot, left to its own devices, will simply continue to grow until it forms a flowering shoot. Unless it is stopped the plant will become unmanageable, but timing is important. Pinching too early may remove the embryo bud along with the leaves. Pinching too late will check the growth of the plant. Wait till the shoot is large enough before pinching out about ¼ in (6–8 mm) of the central tip. Fine-pointed small scissors are ideal for this, but unless they're very sharp they could crush the fine tissue. Experienced growers wait till the shoot is large enough for them to use their thumb and finger nails.

Unless you are simply maintaining or shaping your plant in the early stages of training, don't stop a shoot that doesn't appear to have formed a bud. If you do, you'll delay flowering by the time it would have taken to produce buds on the original shoot.

Fresh growth at soil level shows this plant is ready for pruning.

A young specimen of F. denticulata *after the first stopping*

plant at the same time, to ensure perfectly balanced flowering.

Since the main flush of flowers provides the best display, there's no harm in developing plants that have already produced their first blooms. As long as you provide regular high-potassium feeds, they will continue to flower.

Below: *This specimen of 'Alison Patricia' would not have achieved its splendid shape without careful stopping.*

When buds start to appear on one shoot, you can be almost certain that others will follow on all the growing tips within 7-10 days. As long as one or two shoots are coming into bud, you should stop all the strong growing tips at least eight weeks before your intended flowering date. This will give time for both the new growth and the secondary growth to produce flowers. If the first blooms come after six weeks, the majority will follow about two weeks later.

Experts prefer to allow 60 days for singles, 70 days for semi-doubles and 90 days for doubles to reach their greatest flowering potential after the final stopping.

Do remember that you should make all your stops on a single

Potting

To avoid any possible confusion, I'll begin by defining terms:

* *potting up* involves moving a small plant from the propagator into its first pot

* *potting on* involves moving the plant from a smaller pot to a larger one

* *potting back* involves removing part of the root ball and soil, and then replacing the plant in a smaller pot

* *repotting* involves shaking off soil, then replacing the plant in a pot of the same size, or smaller, with new potting mix.

Above: *The root development here shows the plant is ready for potting on.*

Below: *A magnificent example of a 'Thalia'*

The correct timing and sequence for potting plants is an important aspect of good fuchsia cultivation. As a general rule a small plant grown from a cutting will be potted up into a 2 in (5 cm) pot. When it has achieved a fair amount of growth it should be potted on to a 3 in (7.5 cm) pot. To remove the plant, turn the pot upside down, holding the base of the plant between the first and second finger, and tap the

75

Don't pot on into too large a pot.

pot smartly against the potting bench. This should knock out the plant. If there are very few roots, return it to its original pot. If you can see a definite root system all around the ball of soil, pot on to the 3 in (7.5 cm) pot. If there is a mat of roots, the plant was overdue for potting on. It will probably have suffered, and may flower prematurely.

Pot on regularly as the plant continues to grow, increasing the size of the pots by 1 in (2.5 cm) each time. It's not a good idea to move the plant straight to a much larger pot; potting on from a 3 in (7.5 cm) pot to a 5 in (13 cm) pot, for instance, will probably kill the plant, or at best produce one with too many leaves and not enough flowers.

Potting on may seem like a waste of time, but there is a very good reason for doing it. Unlike the soil outside in your borders, the soil in a pot never encounters real weather, and doesn't have worms to aerate it. The soil around an overpotted plant, confined and constantly watered, will soon lose its air spaces, becoming compacted and sour. The plant's active roots help to keep the soil open and productive.

Although everyone these days uses plastic pots, I still prefer the old-fashioned clay pot. It 'breathes', and it's far easier to manage when plants need water. Plastic pots are less porous, and therefore you have to guard against overwatering, especially if you're using soilless compost. With a clay pot, use the soil-based John Innes compost; with a plastic pot, any proprietary brand is acceptable. Personally, however, I recommend Humber, because it's so much heavier than the other lightweight brands.

Potting bench

I regard a potting bench as essential greenhouse equipment, yet many experienced growers continue to use makeshift benches and tables. This makes potting and repotting unnecessarily difficult. You don't need to be a skilled carpenter, and you don't need expensive materials. If necessary, make your bench collapsible so it can be stored under the staging when you're not using it. A good size is 24 in (60 cm) wide by 18 in (45 cm) deep, and the top should be 0.75-1 in (20-25 mm) thick. For that professional touch (and to keep it clean and tidy) line the base with sheet zinc held in place with copper tacks.

'President Leo Boullemier'

Repotting

Whatever method you're using to cultivate your fuchsias, the key to success lies in one word: 'heat'. As we have seen, there are three basic methods: current growth, biennial cultivation, and normal growth (see page 26). Success with the last method calls for *repotting*. As discussed above, this doesn't involve potting on into a larger pot; instead you shake off the soil, then put the plant into a similarly sized pot, or even a smaller one, with new potting mix. In my opinion this is the only way to produce a specimen plant that's really worth growing — but when should you do it? The answer depends on that key word 'heat'. You *must* keep an eye on the temperature at every stage.

During the winter, keep the soil around the plants slightly moist. In January or February, if the sun is shining and temperatures are relatively high under glass, spray the plants with clean, tepid water. This is better than heavy watering for encouraging the plants to start new growth. When they have made a little growth you can prune them back to any visible pink eyes — provided, that is, that you have frost-free conditions and the temperature is around 38–40°F (3–4°C).

Always apply a slightly firm finger pressure when repotting a plant.

This is a good time to repot the plants and remove as much old soil as possible. You can use the plant's own label to tease out the old soil, using gentle pressure to avoid damaging any fresh young roots. You'll be able to distinguish these by their colour: the old, dead roots will be brown, the new ones white. A little root pruning can be beneficial at this stage, helping to encourage new root growth, but be careful. Older plants may have a long, thick central taproot that will bleed if it's pruned too hard.

Now check the size of the root ball and choose a fresh, clean pot that's just large enough to contain it. Usually this pot will be a size smaller than its predecessor. It may even be two sizes smaller. As a general rule, plants from 6 in (15 cm) pots can be safely accommodated in 4 in (10 cm) pots. Those from 5 in (13 cm) pots will also fit into 4 in (10 cm) pots, or sometimes an even smaller size. With older, established plants it may not be possible to remove all the old soil. In this case take off as much as you can manage, both at the top and underneath, repotting the plant into the same pot.

When repotting it's essential to use fresh, new compost. For outstanding results I recommend traditional clay pots and a soil-based compost such as John Innes No. 2. When you've finished, water the plants well with a very fine pot rose. This will 'settle' the compost, and prevent caking on the surface. You can probably wait up to ten days before you need to water the plants again.

Winter care

Successful winter care depends on two vital factors: the plants must be kept frost-free, and the soil must never be allowed to dry out. Here we are looking at 'normal growth' cultivation, where the plants have flowered the previous summer and need to rest through the winter. Winter care for biennial cultivation calls for slightly different techniques.

The first stage of preparation, ripening the wood, begins in the autumn. Plants should be put outside no later than the end of August; this exposure

should ensure that the wood matures and ripens gradually. Plants will withstand the rigours of winter much better with ripe wood than with young, green, sappy growth. By now you should have stopped feeding, but to help harden off the plants you can give them two or three applications of a high-potassium fertiliser such as potassium sulphate (48.8 per cent K), used at a rate of one teaspoon to the gallon (5 ml to each 4.5 l), or Phostrogen (26.5 per cent K).

In early September you should select the plants you want to

overwinter. Don't grow too many, and discard any that haven't come up to expectation. Storage space in your greenhouse will be at a premium later on.

Gradually withhold water (this will encourage the plants to lose their yellowing bottom leaves), but never let them dry out completely. Don't attempt autumn pruning: the sap is high in the stem, so there's a risk of dieback. Leave major pruning until early spring. You can, however, trim the plants back by removing about one third of the growth made during the summer.

If you're not putting plants outside, you can ripen the wood by leaving the doors and ventilators of your greenhouse wide open until the first frost. Wherever you're keeping your plants, try to maintain the temperature at 40°F (4°C), especially for species and triphyllas. Some plants need to be kept in green leaf, just 'ticking over' through the winter: these include autumn-struck cuttings, whips,

Sequence of pictures left: *Potting back from a tub to a pot ready for the winter:*

1 *The standard in this tub is ready to lift.*

2 *With the standard lifted, the root action is visible.*

3 *The roots have been pruned back ready for potting.*

4 *Operation finished: the standard is now in its winter pot (note the yellow leaves).*

'Dancing Flame'

plants that are being trained (e.g. as standards, espaliers etc.), and plants being grown by the biennial method.

By the end of October or early November the remaining plants will be showing definite signs of needing their winter rest. If any plants haven't shed their foliage, remove all their leaves by hand (*defoliate* them), leaving just the bare stems. Plants can be overwintered safely by keeping them slightly moist at a temperature no higher than 33°F (1°C).

They may even survive a degree or two of frost, provided it doesn't last too long. Even if you can't provide artificial heat, it's still possible to overwinter successfully.

Once you have shaped the plants and defoliated them it doesn't much matter if you store them in the greenhouse, the cold frame, the garage, the shed, or even the spare bedroom, as long as it's *frost-free*. If there's no heat in your greenhouse you can store them under the staging after giving them a good watering; this is essential to maintain moisture during the winter.

Once you've trimmed the plants, lay them down side by side in their pots. Start with the standards, then all the tall, trained plants, and finish with the bushes and shrubs. Pack them all together as closely as possible, one on top of another, on their sides. Cover them completely with sphagnum peat: it should be neither wet nor dry, just nicely moist. Cover *everything* — stems, pots, supports and labels — leaving no part of the plant visible. You can check them once or twice during the winter, but otherwise leave them without heat of any kind until the first week in March. At this point you can unearth them: you should find the plants just ready to be pruned, with young, fresh, pink eyes already showing. This method is almost foolproof, but don't make the peat too wet, or you could have problems with mildew and botrytis.

In a mild winter you can save your plants, wherever they are stored, by covering them with sacking, brown paper, or even newspaper whenever frosts are forecast. Another method is to bury them in an open trench, after treating them as described above for storage under the greenhouse staging.

Pests

One of the fuchsia's outstanding merits is its immunity to most of the pests and diseases that attack other greenhouse plants. As long as you're careful about routine hygiene, most pests can be kept at bay. The best preventative is frequent and thorough spraying of the foliage, especially the undersides of the leaves. Don't wait till you see a pest; make spraying or fumigation part of a regular routine, and you should have no trouble at all.

The following alphabetical list of pests looks rather menacing, but in practice you'll rarely encounter any of them.

Ants
Ants can be very troublesome because they tunnel into the soil and move it about. Generally they prefer a dry atmosphere. By themselves they do little real damage, but they are responsible for the spread of aphids (particularly greenfly) and of mealy bugs.

Aphids
Aphids, both greenfly and blackfly, are the most prolific of all insect pests. They will attack fuchsias both under glass and in the open. Leaf curl may indicate the presence of greenfly. The damage is caused as the insects suck sap from the plant, and their secretion encourages the growth of unsightly, sooty

moulds which block the breathing pores of the plant. Their rate of increase is extremely rapid, so watch any infestation carefully. Any solution of chemicals in water will simply run off an aphid, so you'll need to add a wetting agent or spreader to your sprays.

Ladybirds aren't just nice to look at: they also feed on the aphids that plague fuchsias and many other plants.

Bees
Although bees can't really be described as a pest, their big, clumsy feet can do untold damage to the flowers, especially when they're searching for nectar in the greenhouse. They will bruise and mark blooms enough to render them unfit for exhibition.

As they're daytime visitors, and difficult to control, the only real solution is to cover doors and ventilators with suitable mesh or netting.

These leaves and shoots reveal the ravages of the capsid bug.

Capsid bugs

When your shoots go blind, this is the insect to look for.

Capsid bugs are more likely to attack plants grown outside than those grown under glass. They are green or brown in colour, and look like overgrown aphids ¼-½ in (6-12 mm) long.

They damage the plant by sucking sap from the growing tips: this causes distortion and makes the tip go blind. Other symptoms are brown, blister-like marks on foliage, small holes in the leaves, and distorted leaves.

Caterpillars

Caterpillars are another pest that are usually found outside, but can also be troublesome in the greenhouse.

Many caterpillars are night feeders, and difficult to find. They lay their eggs on the foliage. The larvae will hatch out after a few days or weeks, and can eat voraciously.

Elephant hawk moth caterpillar

The young elephant hawk moth caterpillar is green and brown in colour. At 3 in (7.5 cm) it's large, and it's also terribly destructive. It can devour every leaf on a plant in one night before moving on to the next. These caterpillars also feed on honeysuckle, lilac and petunia; their host plant is the willow herb. The effective control is to pick them off by hand, particularly at night.

Froghopper ('cuckoospit')

This leaf-sucking pest looks like a miniature frog ¼ in (6 mm) long, and leaps when disturbed. To protect itself while feeding,

The enormous caterpillar of the elephant hawk moth is a voracious eater of leaves, and like the adult it is mainly active at night.

81

the nymph surrounds itself with a blob of froth. This is known as 'cuckoospit' because it's usually seen in May, at about the time the cuckoo returns. The froghopper is an outdoor pest, very rarely seen under glass. The remedy is to remove the 'spittle' completely: this can be done by spraying with an insecticide, or even with a powerful water spray.

Fuchsia mite

This extremely serious pest has just reached the UK. It originates in Brazil, and has been threatening the very existence of the fuchsia in California. It is an eriophyid mite that damages the growing points and flowers of fuchsias. The early stages of infection look similar to damage from a heavy aphid infestation, leaving tissues thickened and distorted. If the infection is not checked, it will eventually lead to grotesque malformations of leaves and plant parts, looking similar to peach leaf curl. The mites, just 0.15 mm long, are worm-like with only two pairs of legs. Puckering in young leaves is an early symptom of fuchsia mite: the upper surface becomes blistered and hairy. These symptoms might be mistaken for an attack of mildew. Control is extremely difficult. Even in California little progress has been made towards finding chemicals that can control this pest, and at present no control is available in Britain.

Leafhoppers

Leafhoppers are green insects, smaller than capsid bugs, that look more like beetles than aphids. They're about ¼ in (6 mm) long. Leafhoppers attack fuchsias in much the same way

as capsid bugs. They're rarely seen because they move rapidly when disturbed. Affected foliage has a speckled surface, caused by insects feeding on the underside of the leaves.

Mealy bugs

This is one of the most difficult pests to eradicate, but luckily it isn't common in fuchsia collections. Mealy bugs are white, waxy, louse-like creatures about ¼ in (6 mm) long. They're easily seen, and tend to congregate at the junctions of woody stems, especially on well-established plants. Like other pests, they feed by sucking the sap from the plant, and because they secrete 'honeydew' they also attract the attention of ants.

A tiny leafhopper much magnified — the damage it causes is much more obvious than the insect.

The leaves of this fuchsia have been attacked by spider mites.

Red spider mite

This is one of the most troublesome fuchsia pests, attacking both indoor and outdoor plants. It's really a sucking mite rather than a true spider, though it does spin a web on the underside of the leaves.

Red spider mites like a dry, hot atmosphere; they can't tolerate moist conditions. The mites are extremely small, and sometimes visible only as a sort of rust on the underside of leaves. Infestation weakens the leaf tissues: the leaves turn bronze and yellow, dry up and eventually fall.

This pest tends to be difficult to eradicate from untidy greenhouses, since it will hibernate in litter and in brickwork crevices.

Thrips

These minute insects are just 0.06 in (2 mm) long. They have elongated bodies with four long, narrow, fringed wings. The adults are dark in colour, but the young are a dirty white.

Thrips are very difficult to detect. The simplest way is to place a sheet of white paper under the plant and then shake the plant. Minute thrips will fall onto the paper, where they can be seen as wriggling specks.

This is another insect that thrives in hot, dry conditions and hates the sprayer. Thrips damage leaves by sucking the sap. This bleaches the leaves, often creating a 'pepper and salt' appearance.

In the greenhouse thrips will breed continually if they are not controlled.

Vine weevil

The vine weevil is a flightless, brownish-black beetle with yellow flecks on its wing cases.

These tiny thrips nymphs are virtually invisble to the naked eye, and the adults look no more than wriggling specks — yet they can cause no end of damage if left unchecked.

Below: *Red spider mites make webs like spiders, but like mites they suck the sap from their host plants.*

in the compost at the rate of 1 oz per gallon (30 g per 4.5 l).

Wasps

Wasps may attack flowers, half emasculating them and bruising the sepals and corollas. The workers feed on any sugary substance, and have a taste for fuchsia pollen. The only successful method of control is to destroy the wasps with derris. As with bees, fine mesh or netting over the ventilators and doors will stop them getting into the greenhouse.

The long snout is distinctive. The insect is about 0.4 in (10 mm) long, and its surface is dull matt rather than shiny. The adult is active in late spring and early summer, and eats notches out of the leaves that could easily be attributed to caterpillars. The beetle lays the eggs in the surface soil near the base of the plant, and after the grubs have hatched they start to feed on the plant's root system. This is what does the real damage: vine weevil grubs can eat away an entire root system during the winter and early spring.

The grub is a white, crescent-shaped creature 0.6 in (1.6 cm) long, with a mahogany-coloured head. It curls up into a 'C' shape when unearthed. Grubs are usually found when you are

Vine-weevil grubs and the roots they have practically demolished

repotting in the spring, but can go undetected until the affected plant starts to look decidedly unhealthy. On examination you may find that the root system has already been destroyed. Control is difficult, because both the beetles and the grubs must be dealt with. The best time to eradicate the beetle is in late spring or early summer, before it can lay its eggs. Fumigate the plants, or spray them with HCH or carbaryl. If you suspect the presence of grubs, you can kill them by watering thoroughly with a solution of HCH, diluted as for spraying. Gamma HCH dust is also effective if it's mixed

Whitefly

The waxy white adult whitefly are up to 0.06 in (2 mm) long, and fly off in clouds when disturbed, usually taking cover on the underside of leaves. The immobile scale stage is barely visible. The whitefly is another sucking insect that feeds on the sap and excretes honeydew. This encourages the growth of sooty mould fungi which close up the pores of the leaves. Whitefly are difficult to eradicate. The eggs and the scale stage are immune to pesticides, and the adults must be killed before they breed, since there are constant overlapping generations. Spray or fumigate at 5-7-day intervals until the infestation has been cleared. The control is frequent sprays of bioresmethrin, diazinon, dimethoate, malathion or resmethrin. Fumigate with HCH, or use a malathion aerosol.

Woodlice

These insects have a grey to yellowish segmented body (thorax), and grow up to ½ in (12 mm) long. They roll up into a ball when disturbed. Most woodlice are omnivorous, feeding on decaying matter. They eat holes in leaves and stems, and will attack soil and aerial roots. Woodlice prefer a warm greenhouse, and produce two broods of 50 every year. They are always found where rubbish is left lying about. They can be controlled with good hygiene, and by watering or dusting with HCH. Mixing carbaryl dust in your compost will prevent root attacks.

Whitefly and their eggs — a pest that is very difficult to eradicate

Recommended pest control

Ants	HCH, pyrethrum
Aphids	HCH, Lindane, Sybol 2, Tumblebug
Capsid bugs	HCH, Lindane, malathion , nicotine, Tumblebug
Caterpillars	Derris, malathion, Tumblebug
Leafhoppers	HCH, Lindane, malathion
Red spider mite	Azobenzene smoke, derris, malathion, Sybol 2
Thrips	HCH, derris, Lindane, malathion, nicotine, Sybol 2
Vine weevil	HCH, Lindane
Wasps	derris
Whitefly	HCH, Lindane, malathion, Sprayday, Picket G
Woodlice	HCH, pyrethrum, ant-killer

Diseases

Fortunately very few diseases affect the fuchsia, and the one or two to which it is vulnerable can be thwarted by strict hygiene and cleanliness in cultivation.

Grey mould (*Botrytis*)
This fungal disease is easily identified by the grey, hairy mould it produces. It is most prevalent in winter and spring and can affect any plant, turning stems and leaves brown or black.

To prevent grey mould you should avoid overcrowding your plants, especially when ventilation is poor. Cold conditions with high humidity and little or no air movement are perfect for grey mould; they're also completely wrong for your plants. Use heat or ventilation to move the air, and treat any infection with a fungicide such as benomyl. Benlate is extremely effective; ICI have added activex to their new benlate formula-tion, and claim that it leaves foliage with a natural, glossy finish. Other sprays include captan (Strike), thiram (Hexyl) or, if you prefer a fumigant, tecnazene (Murphy's Pest and Disease Smoke). During the growing period, pay very strict attention to the correct spacing between plants, especially on the staging: not even one leaf should be overlapping with another.

Many of these leaves show the telltale signs of grey mould, known to botanists as Botrytis cinerea.

Rust has become an increasing problem in recent years, and is easily carried in on the wind.

Rust

Rust is another fungal disease; it has always been a problem for fuchsias, and has become an even more serious problem in recent years. Disturbingly, you could bring it in unwittingly on plants bought from some specialist nurserymen. Rust is easy to identify, producing reddish-brown and orange spore patches or pustules on the underside of the leaves which show as black or yellow spots on the upper surface.

The host plant for rust is the willow herb, but spores can be carried on the prevailing wind, or even by bees. Outbreaks usually begin just inside the greenhouse door, or near an open roof light; infection is spread by draughts and air currents.

Rust is a serious problem. It prevents light from getting to the leaves, restricts the amount of food produced, and stunts the growth of the plant. It is very contagious, and spreads rapidly. The only sure-fire cure is to pick off all the affected leaves by hand. For effective control, use Nimrod T from ICI or Plantvax 75 by Uniroyal. Nimrod T is formulated as a liquid for systemic control. It contains bupirimate and triforine, and is an improvement on general garden fungicides containing thiram.

'Padre Pio'

Showing and exhibiting fuchsias

There's nothing difficult or mysterious about cultivating fuchsias for exhibition. You simply grow your plants in exactly the same way as usual, but pay just a little more attention to detail. With care you, too, can achieve the ultimate goal of producing perfect specimen plants.

The daintiness and charm so characteristic of the fuchsia mean that many people are content to grow it purely for their own pleasure. Even so, shows have a vital function. Average enthusiasts have a chance to see the work of experts (and to raise their own standards). They can see new cultivars — and they can demonstrate their own skills to the public and to fellow enthusiasts. Remember that you are there for what you can contribute, not just for what you may expect to receive.

In their natural habitat, as we have seen, fuchsias can produce forms ranging from prostrate ground plants to tall trees. Training is essential to make them manageable for the show-bench. Fuchsias in pots are in their prime during the second and third year of growth; after that, they begin to make heavy wood. It's possible (but difficult) to obtain show plants from current growth. Such plants

need protection and heat to achieve the necessary size, and the growth will tend to be soft, so they'll need more staking and more support. This isn't offensive to the judges, but it is undesirable, because they will be looking for short-jointed plants.

In close assessment, British Fuchsia Society judges can allocate points as shown in the table at the foot of the page.

Standards

A clear, straight stem is the hallmark of a good standard. The plant should have a nicely balanced head with no gaps, but an abundance of bloom. If support is necessary it shouldn't

'Gruss aus dem Bodethal'

British Fuchsia Society allocation of points

General cultivation of plants	6 points
Quantity and quality of blooms	6 points
Foliage	6 points
Presentation	2 points

Standards on display at an exhibition

e out of proportion to the hickness of the stem. The ength of clear stem is measured rom soil level to the point vhere the lowest branch grows way from the stem.

Recommended measurements are given in the section on tandards (see page 34).

Baskets

The judges will look for uniform rowth, with an abundance of lowers covering all sides of the asket. There should be no aps, and no part of the basket should be seen when viewed from any angle at eye level. The top and centre of the basket should be covered with foliage or bloom.

Bushes

Plants that have growth appearing from soil level will score highly here; the emphasis in this class is on vigorous and symmetrical plants. Ideally there should be several stems growing from below soil level, but each pot may contain only one plant.

Most judges will take likely exhibits from the bench, place them on the ground, and look at them from every angle. They will pay particular attention to stakes, canes and ties, which should be unobtrusive, and hidden wherever possible. Foliage should be clean, healthy and above all free from pests and yellowing of the leaves.

89

'Celia Smedley'

Cut blooms

Blooms should be perfect. Premature opening, bruising or fading will all lose points. The colour and shape of the flower should be typical of its cultivar, and it should be fresh. If the pollen has darkened to brown, then the bloom is past its best.

The perfect bloom is described as carrying just a little pollen, enough to attract pollinating insects. There should be four evenly spaced, undamaged sepals; flowers with three or five sepals are not typical of the cultivar. In this class it's very rare to see six perfect blooms; to achieve the freshness so essential to success, I suggest gathering and staging them a few hours before judging.

Single and double blooms

In the single and double classes, judges pay particular attention to entries which contain the wrong blooms. Single flowers are judged by the actual number of petals, which should be four petals only. Catalogue descriptions are ignored. All semi-double flowers should be exhibited in the classes for singles. Some single-flowered cultivars will occasionally throw semi-double blooms, especially if they're overfed.

Don't overlook presentation. In classes that call for more than one pot, think about colour blending. In three-pot classes lift either the back plants or the

 Most successful show-bench plants at national level are large two- or three-year-olds, or grown by the biennial method.

However, you can obtain a successful show-bench specimen on one season's growth if you select a fast, vigorous cultivar such as 'Border Queen', Cambridge Louie', 'Mieke Meursing', 'Shellford' or 'Waveney Green'. You must pay strict attention to the gradual potting-on procedure; the above cultivars would finish in a 5-in (13-cm) or even a 6-in (15-cm) pot.

Above: *'Coachman' in a multi-pot display*

Right: *The show judges with the best fuchsia in the show.*

front ones to produce the right balance. It's no longer regarded as a good idea to 'pop' premature blooms (i.e. to open the buds with the finger and thumb), and the judges can tell that it has been done, so the exhibitor gains no advantage.

Most judges are available after the judging, and you needn't be hesitant about approaching them for advice, guidance and general information. Their aim, after all, is to help all growers improve their standards of cultivation and presentation.

Fuchsia societies

In response to the growing interest in fuchsias there are now flourishing specialist societies in most of the world's temperate countries. By far the largest is the British Fuchsia Society, formed in 1938. Currently it has some 6,000 members, and 300 affiliated societies. The BFS was formed with the object of furthering interest in cultivation. Membership allows free admission to all shows, and free entries on the showbenches. Shows are currently held at London, Manchester (Sale), Loughborough, Plymouth, Swansea, Bournemouth, Bristol, Felixstowe and Harrogate in England, and Linlithgow in Scotland.

You may be interested in joining one of the 200 local specialist societies that have been established all over the UK. All hold regular meetings with lectures, and stage their own independent shows. Details of your nearest society are available from the current Honorary Secretary, R. Williams, 20 Brodawel, Llannon, Llanelli, Dyfed SA14 6BJ, or from the author, Mr Leo B. Boullemier, 1 St Matthews Parade, Northampton NN2 7HE.

There are national societies all over the world. America has two national bodies, both based in California, with a membership of approximately 1,000. The American Fuchsia Society in San Francisco is the international authority for the registration of the fuchsia. The Dutch National Society is the second largest, with over 3,000 members; its week-long national show, held in the open air, attracts up to 50,000 visitors. Other societies can be found in Australia, Austria, Belgium, Canada, Denmark, France, Germany, Italy, New Zealand, Norway, South Africa, Sweden and Switzerland.

Left: *'La Rosita'*

Right: *The oldest fuchsia in Britain, housed in the conservatory of Wallington Hall, Northumberland*

Sources of supply

You may be tempted to buy your fuchsia plants from garden centres. The better garden centres will have a fuchsia section, but in general you'll get better results by buying direct from specialist fuchsia nurseries. Naturally, these also have a much wider range of varieties.

A selection of specialist nurseries is given in the panel.

Lechlade Fuchsia Centre in Gloucestershire: once Britain's leading fuchsia nursery, it was later turned into a large garden centre, and even the fuchsia section there has now been discontinued.

Arcadia Nurseries
Brasscastle Land
Nunthorpe
Middlesbrough
Cleveland
TS8 9EB
Tel: 01642 310782

B. and H. M. Baker
Bourne Brooke
Nurseries
Greenstead Green
Halstead
Essex
CO9 1QL
Tel: 01787 472900

Gouldings Fuchsias
West View
Link Lane
Bentley
Ipswich
Suffolk
IP9 2DP
Tel: 01473 310058

Jacksons Nurseries
Clifton Campville
near Tamworth
Staffordshire
B79 0AP
Tel: 01827 373307

Little Brook Fuchsias
Ash Green Lane West
Ash
Aldershot
Hampshire
GU12 6HL
Tel: 01252 29731

C. S. Lockyer
(Fuchsias)
'Lansbury'
70 Henfield Road
Coalpit Heath
Bristol
BS17 2VZ
Tel: 01454 772219

Kathleen Muncaster
Fuchsias
18 Field Lane
Morton
Gainsborough
Lincolnshire
DN21 3BY
Tel: 01427 612329

Oldbury Nurseries
Brissenden Green
Bethersden
Ashford
Kent
TN26 3BJ
Tel: 01233 820416

J. Pacey
The Nurseries
City Road
Stathern
Melton Mowbray
Leicestershire
LE14 4HE
Tel: 01949 60249

J. V. Porter
12 Hazel Grove
Southport
Lancashire PR8 6AX
Tel: 01704 533902

Potash Nurseries
Cow Green
Bacton
Stowmarket
Suffolk IP14 4AJ
Tel: 01449 781671

J. Ridding
Fuchsiavale Nurseries
Worcester Road
Torton
Kidderminster
DY11 7SB
Tel: 01299 251162

John Smith and Son
Hilltop Nurseries
Thornton
Leicestershire
LE67 1AN
Tel: 01530 230331

94

Index